Written by a man of [barcode: T0163652] to action? First to know ourse..... .... .umm... knows us, not the man or woman shaped by the views and beliefs of others. Second, to rise up in our true identity to make an eternal impact in this world; As Don says, "Who will save the systems? We will." Don challenges us to take our place with the Father; and change history. Don reminds us that our destiny is not created from what is outside, but from the blueprint that He put inside of us. We have to take action now. History will reveal whether we stepped in at this crucial time in our nation to be all He called us to be.

Stephen O'Quinn
President, Perissos Inc; Cofounder, EPIC in Business

In this powerful book, Don Long masterfully reveals the keys to accessing the infinite treasures hidden within us all, empowering us to maximize our fullest potential in this world, with paradigm shifting wisdom and insight.

Duncan Smith
President , Catch The Fire World

In the book of Job, after listening to all the talking heads have their turn at trying to philosophize God's ways, a young man named Elihu stands and in his own words says "I can't stay silent anymore, I waited, I listened, I paid close attention but there is a spirit in man". That is the same spirit and the same burst of wind that comes from Don to redirect a culture who has been led by a passive breeze. I've known Don for many years and I've heard him speak the heart of this book many times and it's challenging concepts never weaken, it only gets stronger. He is a man who desires deeply for every believer in Jesus to recognize who they are according to God's promises and take action and command of their lives in the highest capacity. With these revelations in his pocket, Don has lived what he believes and chases the God who has changed his life completely.

Dan Colvin
Senior Pastor, Center City Church

In the midst of this outpouring, The Lord has raised up voices, prophets that are calling sons and daughters into deeper realms of truth and identity in Him. Don Long is among those who are speaking what the Holy Spirit is doing right now, for this present moment. Don speaks with not only the revelation of heaven but the authority of one who has experienced and walked out the message he carries with unwavering purpose. Don challenges us all to wake up to new dimensions of our identity in Christ.

Sherri Colvin
Senior Leader, Center City Church

THE BLUEPRINT OF GOD

THE BLUEPRINT OF GOD

The Wisdom to Change the World is in You

DON W. LONG

NEW YORK

LONDON • NASHVILLE • MELBOURNE • VANCOUVER

The Blueprint of God
The Wisdom to Change the World is in You

Published in New York, New York, by Morgan James Publishing. Morgan James is a trademark of Morgan James, LLC. www.MorganJamesPublishing.com

ISBN 9781642796858 paperback
ISBN 9781642796865 eBook
Library of Congress Control Number: 2019943720

Cover Design by:
Chris Treccani
www.3dogcreative.net

Interior Design by:
Christopher Kirk
www.GFSstudio.com

Scripture quotations are taken from the King James Version* of the Holy Bible.

Morgan James is a proud partner of Habitat for Humanity Peninsula and Greater Williamsburg. Partners in building since 2006.

Get involved today! Visit
/giving-back

TABLE OF CONTENTS

FOREWORD

T his book is an invitation, it is going somewhere and invites the reader to join in.

I haven't spent a great deal of time with Don, unlike others who have influenced his life and the writing of this book, but I have spent enough time to know that to read the book is to meet the expanded version of the man who I have met. 'Real Don' and 'says it the way it is Don,' offering succinct wisdom and rapid fire bursts of tell it the way it is, all surrounded by supernatural possibilities, biblical insight and identity and destiny discovery keys and tips.

Early in the book I met Don's challenge to leave smallness behind and it definitely came in a 'tell it the way it is' package.

"While we are making excuses and using God as our scapegoat, a secular business person says, "I didn't out work my competition or market well enough" or "I should've gotten more sales, or our strategy could've been

better." Instead of blaming God or the devil, they take responsibility and change the plans and actions they take. He showed me through this that we, in a lot of cases, have been irresponsible with our own gifts and talents. We play the victim and take another trip around the same mountain of playing small."

Don continues by giving us many angles to look at our life's assignment and the opportunities, mindsets, and resources available to accomplish it or them.

I loved this emphasis on not playing life small. I felt challenged and empowered by it, but I particularly loved that this was not just an in the church message. This is a man who has spent his life serving the church while doing kingdom at every opportunity of his life, especially outside of the church.

"The identity of the ecclesia must be reestablished as a culturally-transforming movement that changes our cities from dark to light. We can no longer be ineffective outside of the four walls of the church."

Don has also grasped something which we all need and that is the journey of discovery. Discovery of identity, destiny & dreams amongst other things.

"What He put in you is tied to your destiny and your authenticity. You will be happiest when you are discovering and unpacking the dreams that resonate with your own heart that cause you to come alive inside and out."

I am a great fan of practical advice and keys to application of teaching and I was particularly struck by this simple acronym:

"What if the world is crying out for certain things on the tree of life and that part is hidden in you?

D – Desire of the Father.

R– Realizing the dreams in your heart.

E – Experiencing your capacity to grow into your dreams.

A – Adaptability and pruning that comes with growth.

M – Mastery of your gifts, talents, and abilities. "

I will certainly be borrowing this but also as someone who loves to lead people on the discovery journey this set of questions got my attention.

"What is the big YES in you? What if experiencing your big YES actually shows the world who He is? I call it a divine manifest obsession.

To find pieces of the blueprint in you, ask yourself these questions:

- *What makes you happy?*
- *What makes you smile?*
- *What makes you feel a sense of accomplishment?*
- *What turns you on and lights you up?*
- *What fills your soul?*
- *What feeds you?*
- *What makes you feel free?*
- *What makes you feel frustrated and mad?*
- *What challenges you because you see pain and you want to fix it? "*

I don't remember quoting an author in a foreword as much as I have this time. It was hard not to, these quotes deserve reading twice and applying many times over. Well done Don, its you, its inspiring, its practical, it lifts our hearts and minds to greater things.

I will end where Don ended Chapter 4:

"We must return to the gates of conflict and to the battle for the souls of our cities. Join me in reclaiming our identities as heirs and joint heirs with Him. Our cities, states, and nations are waiting for us, His sons and daughters, to manifest His heart and His answers. I believe He is raising up a group of people that will accept His mission. I'm determined to be one of them. I hope you'll join me."

Reading this demands an answer. Will you join him?

Paul Manwaring
Member of Senior Leadership Team Bethel Church,
living & ministering in Europe
Author: *Kisses from a Good God, What On Earth is Glory*

ACKNOWLEDGEMENTS

Where to begin... I've had so much help and encouragement writing this book.

To my two best friends, Dan Colvin and Stephen O'Quinn, whose help, insights and thought-provoking challenges in unpacking the revelation I received were indispensable to me. Without them, the writings you are reading may have been lost.

To Ericka James and Heather Mize who aided me in putting these insights into a digestible format through their creative writing skills and editing processes.

To my friend Duncan Smith who was willing to be a huge sounding board and challenged me throughout the process to refine it into a work of Art and Action.

To my creative team and publisher whose faith and belief in me gave the courage to complete this project: Joshua A. Smith and Michelle Kulp, Morgan James publishing and your entire team.

Finally, to my wife, Snow, who has always been my biggest cheerleader. Without her love and belief, I would not be the person I am today!

With all my heart and gratitude, I thank all whose hard work and belief made this book possible.

INTRODUCTION

God Had a Dream and He Wrapped Your Body Around It!

One morning in early 2006, I found myself in a ball on the shower floor crying so hard my tears where shooting sideways. Water pounded my body, and it felt as if a heavy weight mashed me to the floor, and I couldn't get up. I laid there not understanding what I was experiencing for what seemed like a half hour, and my mind raced to access what was happening to me. But, I had no frame of reference for anything like this.

From the time my wife and I were in our early twenties, we attended and were part of a local church. We had some great experiences over the years, and saw many signs and wonders. We became part of the Leadership team of that ministry and gave our best to help it grow. The main Leader at this ministry was like a father to me, and we spent a lot of time together over twenty years. I absolutely enjoyed it and received a great foundation in the scriptures from his mentoring.

At the end of 2004, I realized that the very person and place that I had grown up in many ways spiritually was about to change. Although I had learned so much from my mentor, there were things that I started to see that I felt I couldn't embrace and move forward with in my life. These where not legal or moral issues, they centered more around theological differences and certain beliefs about our denominational worldviews. I will leave it at that because to this day I still respect and appreciate everything he did for me and taught me. But the pain and the feeling in my heart wouldn't go away, so after meeting with him many times over several months with no resolve, I decided to resign all my leadership roles and leave the organization that I thought I would be part of forever.

Then, for over a year, I began to unravel spiritually and emotionally. Had I done the right thing for my family and myself? Had I just walked away from what I felt was part of my spiritual destiny on earth? What did I really believe about God? Who am I now without this place in my life? Was the relationship that Jesus had talked about with the Father only for Him, or was it for me as well?

In many ways, I didn't realize how much of my identity I had derived from being part of the organization I had helped to build instead of my identity being built on my relationship with God. This is where all the pain was coming from—I had adapted to the forms and ways of the thing I was part of and that was what defined my personal relationship with

Him. I felt lost and alone not really knowing who the Father was for myself and blaming Him for the pain I had experienced at what seemed like the hands of others, but it was my own lack of healthy boundaries and a twisted form of beliefs around specific insights that I had developed. It's amazing what can change in a moment with God!

At the beginning of 2006, I was introduced to a new set of thoughts on who God was and what He thought about me. One of the thoughts that started to break me free from the emotional pain I was still carrying was God is good, and He was in a good mood, and He loved me, and that I should learn to think for myself about what and why I believe it. That all teaching no matter who taught it had some bones in it. That I needed to learn to eat the meat and spit the bones out. This began to set me free and give a newfound freedom in my life. As these new things started coming to me a new sense of life and purpose began to burn in my heart again. Now back to the shower, as I laid there an intensity of love I had never experienced seem to overwhelm me almost to the point of being breathless, but I didn't want it to end because it was the purest form of love and joy I had ever felt.

When I finally came to myself, I was shaken to say the least. Little did I know that I would have many similar encounters in different places in 2006. At the time, I had no way to explain this to others, but what I came to realize was I had just run into The Love of the Father Himself and He had just introduced me to Sonship with Him including a new level of walking out my relationship with Him as a son.

So it began, and He so marked me with these encounters with Him that I realized how much He not only loves us but wants to do life with us. He started showing and unpacking the very thoughts and heart of what you will read in the coming pages of this book.

I started to realize that we are pre-wired for greatness before we are born by Him, and that He longs for you to Dream with Him and to find and unpack the destiny that He put in you. That through your desires that are from Him, your life here on earth would have eternal impact on those that He calls you to!

Over the last fourteen years, I have studied and continued to read materials that either support or has opened up more thoughts and ways to connect you to your blueprint and destiny. I kid my friends that I have thrown more books away on the subject of personal growth and how that is tied to you full filling your destiny than most people will ever read. I've been on a personal quest to find out how to put the pieces of the puzzle together of my blueprint and find out how to apply my gifts, talents, and abilities to get the most out of me that the Creator put there. It's been and continues to be a lifelong desire to not only manifest my dreams, but to help others find their dreams and, in the process, live a life that's fully alive and free.

This book is broken down into three sections. Section One deals with the major systems of thought in our current world that exist, and how they influence our lives and produce cultural norms whether they be good or bad. For example, the media produced every day through your TV, Internet, and radio continually fill the airways with their particular worldview and influence the masses of people in our nation. The same is true for Hollywood and the movies and shows that are produced as well as the people they call stars that are put forth as an example. These two systems alone produce more cultural shifts and changes in society than most of the other systems of thought combined.

Section Two details the answers and the blueprint within you to change the world around you.

Section Three shows you how to walk out your unique blueprint in a way that allows you to produce answers for the people around you.

Now, we are at the moment that requires action! Do you want to be part of something that changes the world around you for good? Are you ready to find some of the answers the world is crying out for that can only be found in you? You are the Answer for someone and some specific problem in our Nation. You know it's true, and you can feel that you were built for something greater than you are currently living now! The Creator has made you for such a time as this. Don't miss your destiny because of fear or hesitation. I promise you that if you will take this journey with me and discover the DNA of the Father inside of you, the life that will unfold will be almost magical, and you will begin to live fully alive and free! Let the journey begin.

Chapter 1:

GOD'S SYSTEMS

began receiving insights and revelations about systems of thought from the Lord many years ago and in 2016 I started having a real burden to see change in our nation. I realized that we had drifted far away from our Godly heritage and foundation. This book is the product of those insights. For the first twenty years of my life, I didn't know the systems even existed. Over the last decade, I've learned how many of our lives are controlled by these systems no matter our personal beliefs.

My journey began in 2016 when I heard the Father say, "Teach my church to be more worldly." I immediately laughed and replied, "This is going to go over like a lead balloon." Then, I started receiving small insights and snapshots of what He was saying and what He was trying to convey. Over several weeks, He began to unpack what He was trying to teach me. He led me to four or five main foundational scriptures from which I began to write, and then many more followed.

The main scripture that we will focus on is John 3:16-17. As I read and studied it, I noticed that 'world' was included in this scripture four times and humanity, the 'whosoever,' only once.

> *For God so loved the **world**, that he gave his only begotten Son, that **whosoever** believeth in him should not perish, but have everlasting life. For God sent not his Son into the **world** to condemn the **world**; but that the **world** through him might be saved.*
> – John 3:16-17

The Lord was showing me that the word "world" is translated as cosmos, which means orderly arrangement and/ or world system. These systems of orderly arrangement were created to give us insight into the Father's thoughts and ways for us.

Proverbs 8:2-3 tells us that wisdom, which is God's thoughts and ways, is set at the highest place in the city. She, wisdom, cries out at the gates at the entry of the city or nations.

Proverbs 9:1-3 says that wisdom has built or hewn out her seven pillars, and wisdom is at the very highest place in the city or nations.

In these two references in Proverbs, when wisdom or God's systems of thoughts are over a nation, it brings His best to us and for us. When Adam fell in the garden, he gave his authority to the enemy, and Satan began to implement his corrupted wisdom over the high places and the gates, which is an entry into every city or nation according to Proverbs 8:2-3 and Proverbs 9:1-3.

Foundations for Wisdom

The seven pillars referenced in Proverbs 9:1-3 are the foundations for wisdom. The pillars represent the systems or primary influences over our world. While there may be others, these are the main systems:

1. **Government**
2. **Communication**
3. **Commerce**
4. **Education**
5. **Arts**
6. **Family**
7. **Religion**

The systems of thought are similar to the message given to two of the largest youth movement leaders in the 1970s—Bill Bright, founder of Campus Crusade for Christ, and Lauren Cunningham, founder of Youth with a Mission. The Lord gave the message to them separately, and they came together to share what they received. When they compared notes, they realized that as a nation we would always be discipled by the small percentage of people who propagate and dictate the narrative of the thoughts at the high places. Whether it's the Father's wisdom or it's the corrupted version, one will stand guard at the gates. Over the past decade, I began to realize that nations are discipled by a small percentage of people who rule the systems.

Less than 3% of the population controls our nation's culture, and we are being discipled by the thoughts or "mind molders" in the different systems. For example, in the United States, the legislative branch (Congress and the Senate) make federal laws that we all must obey or suffer the consequences; yet the members of the legislative branch make up less than 1% of the population. The elected officials are at the place of power and proximity at the gates at the top of our legislative system where they decide the laws by which we must live.

What I began to realize is that God's people, in many ways, have left the room or have abandoned the gates of our legislative system as well as many other systems. As a result, we are not included in the conversations that are shaping these essential and critical systems that affect our lives every day. We have abdicated our responsibility that God gave us in the mandate of the Great Commission, as described in Matthew 28:16-20 which gives us the responsibility to disciple and teach Nations the thoughts and ways of the Kingdom of Heaven.

*And Jesus came and spoke to them, saying, "All authority has been given to Me in heaven and on earth. Go therefore and **make disciples of all the nations**, baptizing them in the name of the Father and of the Son and of the Holy Spirit,*

> ***teaching them to observe all things that I***
> ***have commanded you****; and lo, I am with you*
> *always, even to the end of the age." Amen.*
> – Matthew 28: 16-20

John 3:16-17 has a much broader implication for the Great Commission than we have ever realized. God mentioned the systems, or 'world,' four times and humanity, the 'whosoever,' only once on purpose. Yet, I've never heard this taught.

The World's Systems

The world's systems were created by God Himself to be a blessing to humanity and to teach and convey His ways of doing things. Man is God's highest form of creation, and we are meant to be sons and daughters of the Father Himself—a family. He knew that if He had the systems of thought in place that originated from Him and His heart, the systems would produce His ways, wisdom, and understanding of doing things. His systems were to be infused with His DNA and always produce life for humanity. They would be living and breathing with the Creator's breath and life in them.

These systems existed prior to Adam (see Ezekiel 28:16). Lucifer oversaw some system of trading, commerce, or business that existed from Heaven to earth before corruption was found in him. In other words, Heaven was and will be a very productive place when we get there. We probably will be surprised by how busy it is. He is the Creator. What do creators do? They are continually creating. Part of our dress rehearsal here on earth will prepare us to rule with Him, and we will have a role in the Father's family business.

Isaiah 61:3-7 teaches us that the anointing fixes and mends people, heals them, sets them free, and causes humanity to find freedom in Christ and His Word. But the anointing is more than a mending station or a hospital. If you read Isaiah 61:3-7 closely, you will see that the very people who were healed actually become the people He uses to restore and rescue cities, rebuild old ruins, restore what is broken, fix and repair what is needed. Once we are rescued, we often become—and should become—a catalyst to rescue others.

As I have matured in the Lord, I have realized that He wants us to be like Him. He wants us to become champions and rescuers of the world and the people in it so that what He paid for with His blood can be restored back to the original state. This might stretch what you think is possible. 1 John 4:17 says, "As He is, so are we in this world." This scripture means that He expects us to take responsibility for what He has given us to restore. We are to fix what has been broken, heal and repair our communities, including the people and the systems to transform our world. Who will save the systems? We will.

The Great Commission

Our place in history is much bigger than we have believed. We have been given a powerful Great Commission by the Master Himself that is three-pronged:

1. To disciple nations

2. Save and repair the systems
3. Get every soul saved

We have mainly focused on one-third of the Great Commission—saving people. Of course, this is paramount and should not be overlooked. However, I'm writing this book to inspire us to be bold and step into the arena of the other two-thirds of our commission that have mostly been talked about, but not acted upon. He has given us everything we need in order to do it. The question is, will we accept our commission? Or will we continue to be under the world's culture instead of Kingdom culture? God so loved the world's systems that He gave His only son to save them. It is time for us to join Him in the full commission.

I picture the systems as organic, fluid in nature—producing through them what I would call the prevailing heart attitude, or the spirit of who controls them, whether it be light or darkness. They were intended to be light from the Father's heart. The Father intended His thoughts and ways to flow through the seven systems, through His wisdom and His DNA implanted in each of them. The Holy Spirit was to be the prevailing spirit over them, and His people would be free to disciple the nations through these systems. We are His ambassadors of light to the world and should be stepping in and restoring and repairing what has been broken. If we don't propagate His ways over the places of influence through our delegated authority from the Father and Jesus, we will allow darkness in the systems to rule over our nations (see Proverbs 8:2-3, Proverbs 9:1-3).

The Father is saying that as we step into our calling to rescue and restore the systems of the world (business, family, education, art, mass communications, entertainment, government, and religion) as He intended in the beginning, He will teach us His ways. The systems themselves carry His DNA and His organic presence throughout each of them. Education would teach us His ways. Business would be done the way God wants it to be run. Government would be run with His thoughts and heart. There would be an organic movement operating throughout these systems because the true DNA of the systems is from the Father. The original intent of the Father was that His DNA, in seed form, would produce life, happiness, justice, and righteousness in each one of the systems for His creation. These systems would become living breathing organisms that distribute His will through them.

You may think this sounds like a daunting task, but it is deeper than that. It speaks to the very nature and purpose of our creation. Why were we created? We were created to be champions in the systems for the Father. Anything less falls short of who we are made to be in Christ. Let's look at the grace of God that gives us all we need in order to be powerful in this life.

The Power of Grace

Grace was given to us to overcome sin, and it was also designed to empower us to become sons and daughters of the King with the ability to rule with Him in this life. We don't realize that grace is much more powerful than we have thought. Grace not only has the power to transform us, but to transform the world and the systems of the world. Grace is the powerful state of His presence that brings the Father's supernatural ability on us and through us to do great exploits in the earth in which we live today, as stated in Daniel 11:32, "The people who know their God shall be strong, and carry out great exploits."

Grace gives us the power to step into our culture, in whatever state it is, and change it. An example of this power is the apostolic movement that started in the early church in the book of Acts that continues to this day. In many ways, the apostolic power of grace to transform cities and nations has been replaced by an inward focus of trying to put Band-Aids on our sins and weaknesses, not truly appropriating the grace of the Father in our personal lives. Failing to find out who we really are in Christ and walking in our full inheritance has been a ploy of the enemy since the beginning to keep us from redeeming the systems of the world.

Who are you and what is your inheritance? WE ARE KINGS AND PRIESTS. WE ARE ROYALTY! We are sons and daughters of the King, and we have the power of the Kingdom in our hands to accomplish all that He has called on us to accomplish. If we believe that sin and weakness define who we are, we nullify the full power of Jesus' blood and the price He paid for us and the world. We will never be able to break free from the enemy's grasp to become the true champions the Father made us to be.

We are new creatures created in Christ Jesus. We are created in Him, the Father. We have to stop focusing on who we were in the past and focus only on who He has made us to be in Christ: one who is entirely complete through His power and grace. It's all about us starting to realize that God works with us and does things through us—imperfect people. Right? Actually, the truth is that we are perfect through the new creation. This part of us is perfect. We have a body and soul that must be renewed, but the endless possibilities of the Kingdom are within us, and as we focus on Him, we will transform into His image and likeness in our lives.

Transformation comes through focusing on Him and His glory and not on our weaknesses and ourselves. Anytime we focus on us instead of seeing ourselves being one with Jesus and the Father (John 17:22), we will either live unaware of our significance to change the world or in a state false humility—which keeps us in a mindset that is more fit for an orphan instead of a Son or Daughter of the King. After being born again, we shouldn't focus on our weaknesses at all. We should focus on the finished work in us, and from there, we will walk out this glorious salvation. This is not to say that if we need help dealing with certain things in our lives, we should not seek out ministry for healing or counseling. However, I am providing a word of caution not to dwell in that place. We need to seek help that supports us and points us back to our true identity in Christ and teaches us to lean into the Holy Spirit as our teacher and comforter. We can continue to live life from the broken state, or we can break free through continually having encounters with the Father. As He grows us up in the process of life, the things that need healing or counseling will fall off, and transformation will take place.

Even if we sin, we have an advocate with the Father— Jesus. So, get up. Get going. Don't let anything in your life keep you from living the life God has placed within you. One of my spiritual mentors, Bill Johnson, says, "I don't do endless introspection because all I find is me, and it depresses me." In other words, you become what you focus on and what you behold. 2 Corinthians 3:18 says, "But we all, with open face beholding as in a mirror the glory of the Lord, are changed into the same image from glory to glory, even as by the Spirit of the Lord." This verse talks about being transformed into the glory of God by focusing on Him, not yourself.

You may say that this can't happen until He comes back—that we can't help restore the earth and people, in large part, before He comes back. If that were true, then Jesus gave us a false mandate in the Great Commission. He left us on earth to execute His mandate and I believe He is not coming back until we have completed our mission. So, I'm going after it with all I have and with all my heart. We can win the nations and systems back from evil and set people free in the process. After all, isn't that what the anointing is for? Isaiah 61:3-7 talks about setting people free, and those same people will be the restorers of cities and repairers of breaches and they will rebuild nations. That's the promise. So, I'm not waiting. I'm moving because He said, "Go." We need to be moving because He has given us His mandate. It's interesting that God's systems aid us in life and they were already in place and created for us. Genesis 1:31 says that everything was created and then He put Adam in the garden. All that we need in order to live was put in place before we were ever created.

The systems were corrupted because of Adam's fall, but Jesus won it all back through His death, burial, and resurrection. He destroyed the power of death and restored us to our original state before the fall. He has given us His power and authority and has given us the keys to the Kingdom to reign in this life in His stead until He returns. As we restore and rescue the systems, we will begin to get the Father's best again through them. I find it mind-boggling that we have missed this. Proverbs 8 and 9 are full of what wisdom looks like in the world's system. Here are a few examples that show us what wisdom at work can do to restore the world:

- Proverbs 8:2 says that wisdom places us at the top of the mountain.
- Proverbs 8:4 says that wisdom gives us an understanding heart.
- Proverbs 8:6 promises that we will bring forth excellence.
- Proverbs 8:9 says that wisdom gives us clarity.
- Proverbs 8:2 promises inherited wealth.
- Proverbs 8:30 promises to give us insight into being a master artist or craftsman.
- Proverbs 9:14 gives us a seat at the highest place in the city.

These systems in their original state were put into place to reveal His heart, ways, and glory and expose all of humanity to Him. Their redeemed expression of the systems will cause people to see Him so that all men and women can taste and see that the Lord is good, giving them a chance to choose Him and His rich goodness toward them. The blueprint for life is in the Word of God itself. I hope to unfold a piece of it that has been left untouched so that you can learn how to be radically successful and be called to your destiny through the insights that He has given you.

The Apostles

One of the insights we gain from how Jesus set up the early church is that He instructed His disciples to convert culture. He could have used world-changers, prophets, or champions. But the title He gave them was Apostles, a Roman term—not Christian or Jewish. The word "apostle" describes someone much like an ambassador from a military occupation who would go in and convert a culture that had just been conquered to the ways of Rome. The Roman Apostle was in charge of converting the city's thought and culture to Rome's. It's interesting that Jesus used a worldly term to describe what His disciples are called to do—bring the Kingdom of Heaven and convert cities to the culture of the Heavenly Kingdom.

In this book, I hope to convey an understanding of how to be in the world—true to how we are commissioned by Christ as His apostles. The early church provides an example of being true apostles. Through their authority and power in

Christ, they shook up entire cities. Acts 17:6 reads, "...these who have turned the world upside down have come here too."

The early church had three major signs of being an Apostle:

1. **Power and Authority**: Within the first few chapters of the book of Acts, nearly 8,000 people were saved, and two people died because they lied to the Holy Ghost. Great fear fell on everyone, and the Apostles moved with great power and authority to fill entire cities with the doctrine of the Kingdom. Jesus Himself said that it only takes a little bit of leaven of Kingdom to leaven the whole lump.

2. **Filling cities with the doctrine of the Kingdom:** Within a few weeks, the religious leaders in charge of Jerusalem brought John and Peter before them. They had already spoken to them several times in this passage saying, "Don't speak in this name anymore." Acts 4:18 and 5:28 say that the leaders looked at John and Peter and said, "You have filled this city with your doctrine." My hope in writing this book is that we (YOU) would fill our cities, communities, states, and nations with the doctrine of the Kingdom. The Kingdom of God is His rule and it reigns over the world systems themselves, including the seven pillars, or systems. Isaiah 2:1-4 says that the mountain of the house of the Lord will be over all of the other mountains.

3. **Turning their world (and systems) upside down**: Acts 17:6 states that those who turned the world upside down are now coming into our city. The rulers of these cities were not in favor of the Apostles coming into their cities. This was not a positive statement. The early church had a reputation of turning cities and nations upside down. Why? Because they were carrying the power and authority that Jesus had given them in the Great Commission (see Matthew 28:18-21). The power of the Holy Spirit that was upon them would challenge and disrupt any other principalities in the region of that city that were not of God. Many times, these principalities and powers would be attached to human beings. Then, the people in the cities would manifest and rise up and reject the Apostles. As the modern day apostolic movement, our mission is to stand in His power and His light until darkness yields.

Culture

I believe the church has been ineffective in winning culture and the war over our cities, communities, and states. We have lost the battle for every system for which Jesus died. If we want to save the systems again, we must return to the prototype of the early church and convert culture once again to the Kingdom, and save it from the evil and darkness that prevails in it now.

We will explore in the coming chapters that the wisdom to not only change the world but to establish Heaven's culture like the early church did lies in each of us. When we discover our DNA from the Father that makes us unique, individually and corporately, we will begin to unpack answers for Nations. Our mandate from the Father is to rescue and restore our world. Isaiah 61:4 says, "And they shall rebuild the old ruins, they shall raise up the former desolations, And they shall repair the ruined cities, The desolations of many generations."

It's time for the heirs to take back the high places where the gates, or openings of influence of the cities, are located. The Word of God says that the gates of hell shall not prevail against us (see Matthew 16:17-19). Yet the gates of hell currently control the top of all the systems in our society. The gates of influence sit at the top of the systems of influence that disciple our society. According to Proverbs 8:3, these gates are at the entry of the cities, and whatever is let into the nation's gates will govern the systems of thought.

In Malcolm Gladwell's book, *The Tipping Point*, he says that only 3-5% of a population is required to create a tipping point or shift. These 3-5 % must be at the right proximity (at the top or close to it) to make a shift in the systems. It is time for the believers to become the 3-5%, or convert the 3-5% who currently sit in the gates to the Kingdom of our Lord. It is time to take back that for which the King Himself paid. The clarion call is to start and move as an apostolic people once again to restore anything in our cities that is not in tune with the Father's values. We need to convert our culture to the Kingdom of Heaven through influence and leadership. We will unpack the Father's thoughts and ways on this in the coming chapters.

The spirit of darkness should not be seated in high places in our cities. We need to reestablish our identity as a royal priesthood, a holy nation within our nations, and take back the gates of influence in the systems. When we do this, we will be able to extend the effectiveness of being the church once again. We will truly be the ecclesia—the called-out ones. When you see Him, you know who you are, and you'll be successful in leading, championing, and serving the systems of the world.

The Kingdom is advanced through influence, not imposition or by forcing people to believe. The task is to become a people who have answers, influence, and solutions for the world's questions. As we love the world and solve their problems, the world will come to know how wonderful our Father is and want Him.

The covenant we are a part of through the inheritance is the promise that was given to Abraham, the Father of our faith.

> *Now the Lord had said unto Abraham, Get thee out of thy country, and from thy kindred, and from thy father's house, unto a land that I will show thee: And I will make of thee a great nation, and I will bless thee, and make thy name great; and thou shalt be a blessing: And I will bless them that bless thee, and curse him that cursed thee: and in thee shall all families of the earth be blessed.*
> – Genesis 12:1-3

These scriptures also remind us of our inheritance:

- Galatians 3:29 says that if we are in Christ, we are Abraham's seed and heirs according to the promise.
- Galatians 3:7-8 says to "know ye therefore that they which are of faith, the same are the children of Abraham. And the scripture, foreseeing that God would justify the heathen through faith, preached before the gospel unto Abraham, saying, In thee shall all nations be blessed."

The promise is about nations. Jesus himself is called the Desire of Nations.

> *And I will shake all nations, and the*
> *desire of all nations shall come: and*
> *I will fill his house with glory, saith*
> *the Lord of hosts.*
> – Haggai 2:7

Finally, we see the Great Commission in Matthew 28:19-20 that our commission is to nations.

> *Go ye therefore, and make disciple of*
> *all nations, baptizing them in the name*
> *of the Father, and of the Son, and of the*
> *Holy Ghost: Teaching them to observe*
> *all things whatsoever I have commanded*
> *you: and, lo, I am with you always, even*
> *unto the end of the world. Amen.*

Identity

We are called to be sons and daughters and princes and princesses of nations. If we really let that sink in, we would stop playing small. We are called-out ones—the ecclesia— to govern at the gates with the Father's heart that is good. We are supposed to inherit nations and serve with His heart, which is always good toward people.

We must settle in our hearts that the Father is good, in a good mood, and that He likes you and other people. When I heard Bill Johnson say these words in 2006, it changed my life and my relationship with the Father forever. I started having encounters with the Lord (my wife did as well). It was as if God had moved into our house, and He didn't leave for an entire year. He showed up randomly, and His presence sometimes would incapacitate me. This became usual in our home, and anywhere else we went for that matter.

At the time, I had no one to explain it to me. I was raised by a spiritual father who is a Doctor of Divinity. I have seen many signs and wonders in my life, but always in the context of church and ministry. These encounters had nothing to do with either, and I found myself in a new territory that neither my wife nor I had ever visited. Then, two major mentors, Bill Johnson and Lance Wallnau, came into my life and provided me with the language to understand what was happening to me, which began to change me forever. I realized that God was doing something new—a new wine skin was being formed in this generation in a way that I had not experienced. As I continued to have these experiences, I now had mentors who could wrap thought and understanding around them.

One of the main changes that resulted from my season of encounters was the Father instilling in me that I was His son. My identity was forever changed. I realized who I was and that the identity I carried wasn't dependent upon me, but on what Jesus did for me. Jesus asked the disciples, "Who do men say I am?" Then He asked, "Who do you say I am?" He asked the second question because their identity was in who they saw Him to be. He was not trying to get them to understand who He was, but who they were in Him. This was directly tied to their identity.

What you think about God is the most important thing about you. When Jesus left us in charge as the ecclesia, He intended for us to govern and rule in this life with His mandate for people—that is to seek, save, disciple, and transform lives. In modern day church, we have reduced the ecclesia down to saving people, attending church on Sunday, and participating in conferences. These all have great value, but there is so much more. This was not the apostolic movement Jesus had in mind. Jesus' desire is that we govern and serve in his stead with the heart of the Father, and that we release through the seven systems His ways, wisdom, and thoughts about life and society itself.

We were meant to be salt, light, and leaven of the Kingdom to the spheres and systems of influence. We were called individually, as well as corporately, so that His influence would be released through the ecclesia. The identity of the ecclesia must be reestablished as a culturally-transforming movement that changes our cities from dark to light. We can no longer be ineffective outside of the four walls of the church. We have to step into the grand plan the Father has for our lives and fulfill our Commission to transform the world.

Genesis 3:1-6 talks about Eve being tempted by the serpent and about not eating from the tree of knowledge of good and evil. It wasn't about the tree. It was about her identity. He already knew that she was like God and made in His image. You'll also see this in the temptation and test of Jesus in the wilderness in Matthew 4:1-4. The first challenge was "If you are the Son of God, you'll change the stones to bread." It was about His identity, not the stones.

If we don't get back to the original place where we were destined to be in the Father, none of this message will matter because without knowing who we are, we won't have the power and confidence to go out and change the world. We have to begin seeing ourselves as one with the Father and joint heirs with Jesus Himself. We are royalty. As sons and daughters of the King, we are part of the solution the world needs to see, ambassadors in this life with and through His power.

All attacks on our lives begin with questions about our identity that come from the anti-Christ. When we lose our identity, all other losses are automatic. Losses show up mainly as fear, confusion of who we are, or being ashamed of ourselves. Shame leaves you with a loss of confidence to do life effectively. In life, there are only two states: empowerment or disempowerment. One is from the Father, the other is from the world. Loss of your identity will force you to live in a continual state of disempowerment that causes you to look at the world through a victim or orphan mindset. If you are empowered, looking at the world through your identity allows you to view the world as the Father sees it, with the power to influence and change the world.

Before I move to the next chapter, I want to leave you with this thought: the early Apostles went into the cities with the intention to disrupt current culture, because at that time all cultures were without Christ. They moved in authority and power so that people would be converted. Then, they would bring in a community of believers and reinforcements to disciple and transform the entire city into one of Kingdom thought. They would raise up elders that were in the ecclesia who would then be charged with establishing governing thoughts, ways, and laws that would honor the Father. The whole culture, in many ways, would be under the auspice of the Kingdom. This was done through favor, influence, and leadership by serving the cities with God's best. It wasn't intended to be done through imposition, but through influence and serving. This is what God wants to reestablish through us today—a modern-day apostolic movement that transforms our communities, cities, states, and nations through us having the Father's answers for the world's problems.

Chapter 2:

THE ANSWER–FINDING HIM AND YOURSELF

This chapter wasn't originally going to be in this book, but I woke up in the middle of the night and heard two words: "The answer." What you are reading came out of that statement. Until we can get our identity back and understand what identification really means from His perspective, we won't discover and access the glorious promises that have already been given to us. Now, through His finished work, you are everything Jesus is. Focus on Him and nothing else. Don't focus on any area in your life that you don't measure up yet because of your mind or flesh. Focus on the finished work. His grace is sufficient.

The answers to the questions that the world is looking for and crying out for already exist within you. Those asking and crying out are waiting for you to find your place. The answers of the ages flow out of the Father into you. All of you flows into all of Him; where you end and where

He begins should be indistinguishable. This is what the new creation, being born again, and being one with the Father should look like. This oneness is what Jesus wanted for us to experience in Him and the Father. His desire was that we would be one with the Father like He was (see John 17:22). He wanted this so much that He gave His life so that you and I could taste and live life with complete clarity about our identity.

Identification

The work of identification, oneness in the Father through Jesus, has been lost in our modern era of Christianity. Jesus identified with every part of who we are. He identified with every ungodly trait, sin, infirmity, and affliction—past, present, or future. He identified with every piece of the darkness in humanity. 2 Corinthians 5:21 says, "He became sin that we might become righteousness." The Father loved us so much that He was willing to send His son and put everything—past, present, future, sin, darkness, corruption and whatever existed in our unredeemed states—upon Him so that everything that He was, we would become. 1 John 4:17 states that "as He is now in His resurrected state, so are we in this world." He nailed everything that would keep us tied to eternal separation from Him and the Father to His cross and removed the handwritings against us forever so we would forever be like Him (see Colossians 2:14-15).

In his book titled *Identification: Romance to Redemption*, E.W. Kenyon talks about our oneness with the Father and what Jesus paid for us— the legal side of our redemption. I read his book in my early days as a believer, but didn't really understand the full meaning of identification; I now understand the answer is oneness with the Father, and from that place we have answers for which the world is longing. I have heard the salvation side of identification preached in many ways, and most believers absolutely agree with it, or we wouldn't be born again. Without Jesus and what He did, we are lost forever.

The other part of this message of His finished work has been lost. It has been re-written to accommodate a plethora of doctrinal beliefs developed by well-meaning people to try to explain what He did so people can attempt to understand it. In most cases, this message has lost its power through incomplete teachings and understanding. The other side of the greatest story ever told is of the Father not only rescuing us from separation from Him, but putting us in a seat next to Him where we become everything that Jesus is now in the resurrected state in this life (see 1 John 4:17).

With one last breath, Jesus said, "It is finished." At that time and with those words, we were given access to all the Father had. Because of the finished work, now we are one with the Father and Jesus. John 17:22 says that we are now a son and a daughter with equal rights to Jesus as a joint heir. If you read Galatians 3:7-9, 3:14 and 3:29, you will see that through this relationship, we have not only been made joint heirs (see Romans 8:17) and sons and daughters of Him, but also have received the fullness of the Abrahamic covenant and all that comes with it.

To be a joint heir means to be equal in accessing anything and everything the Father has. We are joint heirs seated with Him. As He is, so are we in the world here and now—not the one to come, but now. We are ambassadors now representing another Kingdom with the same authority and power mentioned in Matthew 28:18-20. You have received the keys to the Kingdom now, not in Heaven—right now. Everything in the Abrahamic covenant is now yours. These promises include:

- Like Abraham, we are to be fathers and mothers of nations (Genesis 12:1-3).
- We have been given the power to obtain wealth (Deuteronomy 8:18).
- Blessings will come upon us as we follow the voice of the Father (Deuteronomy 28:1-14).

These are just a few promises that belong to you. Yet until you know them and have your own encounters with the Father that drive them down into your heart, you will keep looking for the answers in all the wrong places: outside of yourself in the world, church, books, success conferences, etc. Use these avenues to learn and aid you in your journey, but until you start truly realizing who you are in Him and who He is in you, these tools will not have the impact you want in order to change and transform the world around you. Trust me, I've been a life-long student of the Word, as well as in the world. I've thrown more books away trying to find the silver bullet than most people will ever read.

The Answer is Within You

Can I say that again? The answer is within you. All that you need is inside of you right now through the finished work of Jesus. Because of complete identification with Him, He became what we were (sin), so we could become all He is now (wisdom, righteousness, sanctification, redemption—see 1 Corinthians 1:30). Christ's wisdom has been made wisdom to us. There is no answer He doesn't have. Now you have access to the wisdom of the Creator Himself who created the universe. There is nothing the Father can't do, fix, restore, or reform through you. Most believers track with me until the last words "through you," and then I lose most of them because we don't understand the full work of identification.

Let me give you an example from a story that can have a significant impact on our lives today if we choose to believe that the Father wants to be in this powerful relationship with us. Remember that we are sons and daughters of Abraham as it says in Galatians 3:6-9. In Genesis 18:16-19, we see that the God of the universe, Creator of all, makes a statement that is staggering and telling of His work through the cross. He, being the trinity—God the Father, God the Son, and God the Holy Spirit—have this conversation: "Should we destroy Sodom without telling Abraham about it?" Why would the God of the universe, who is perfect in everything He does, need to talk to a man or even, consider it before He moves? The scripture goes on to describe how Abraham negotiated or influenced God on whether He would destroy Sodom. Let's pause there for a moment. You heard that right. God was willing to be influenced by man.

Let me give you one more example to solidify this point. We can all tell the story of Jesus' first miracle of turning water into wine (John 2:1-10). But let's dissect the story carefully. Mary realizes during the wedding feast that all the wine was gone. Do you think Jesus also knew the wine was gone? Mary tells Jesus to provide more wine. Jesus' first response was basically an attempt to tell His mother "No," by saying it was not His time. So, Jesus knew there was no wine, did not plan to provide more wine, and basically told his mother "No." We know from scripture that Jesus only did what the Father wanted Him to do. So, the Father was also aware and said "No" to Mary. But that was not the end of the story. Mary kept pressing and told the servants to do whatever Jesus tells them to do. She did not accept "No" as the answer and influenced the Father to have Jesus turn the water into wine.

Promises and Inheritance

As sons and daughters of the Father, we have the same access as Abraham and Mary—the access to the promises, inheritance, levels of influence to change the world, to champion what is in your heart from Him, to rescue, restore, reform and fix what is broken and undone. You probably didn't realize you were that powerful because it hasn't been taught. But it is so, or the Word of God and what Jesus did isn't true.

Since having a life-changing encounter in 2006 with the Father, I've been on a quest to explore our full privileges as sons and daughters. This quest continues even as I write this book. Ninety percent of believers I've seen have an incomplete understanding of the new covenant and what belongs to us. Most of us are still praying for that which He has already given us access to. All the promises to us in Him are "Yes" and "Amen" according to Paul's writings. This inheritance can now be accessed through faith and patience. We don't need to pray for what we have already inherited. We don't have to go after it and pursue the Father's heart because we already have it. **We don't have to play small, with false humility to get it. It is already done. The undervaluation of ourselves and the false humility that has been adopted because of religion has neutered and castrated our identity.**

The answers the world is crying out for aren't being accessed because there is a lack of understanding of being one with the Father and Jesus. This oneness gives us a seat at His table to communicate with Him to change the course of history, just like Abraham. We have been made royalty because of what Jesus did. We are sons and daughters of the King. Until we are delivered from the slavery of men's traditions and religious beliefs that oppose who we are in the finished work, we will not get the answers for which the world is crying out. I believe John 14:13 when Jesus said, "Whatever you ask the Father in my name, He will give it." The key has to do with us accessing the promises and inheritance that have already been provided for us through Christ by understanding our true identity in Him.

It is time to ask, "How do I access my inheritance Father?" Most people's prayer life is built around asking Him for what is already theirs. My friend, Dan Colvin, asked me, "How do you get the promises and inheritance?" The Word tells us that you receive them through faith and patience. All faith is birthed out of desire that is inside of you through the DNA of the Father. As you grow and mature in Him, desires will bubble up in your heart and then you can go after the thing that He is highlighting in you.

When you see a promise that's for you in the Word, start meditating on it and muttering it as it says in Joshua 1:8, "praying into it and declaring that it belongs to you." In that process, the Father directs you on how to receive the promise. He's a good Father. Sometimes He may reveal some things in us that must change in order to prepare us to receive the promise. Just like you wouldn't give your five-year-old the car keys, He won't just release the keys and promises either. Through your relationship with Him, He will help you grow into what it takes for Him to release His promises to you.

I will tell you how the process of accessing the promises works for me. You will probably have a different process because you are a different son and daughter, and He reveals Himself to each of us through a unique and personal relationship with Him. This is how my process has worked since my encounter with the Father in 2006. Before then, most of what I prayed for was already mine. When I realized this wasn't a way that a son should pray, I changed. I don't look for answers until He highlights something He wants to talk about through a word, vision, something bubbling up inside of me, or something someone says that sparks my attention. At that point, I pursue Him for more insight.

If I see a promise or a piece of inheritance that I'm not yet accessing, then I will begin to mediate and declare it as mine because He has provided it for me in the finished work. I then remain open to how He wants me to receive it or obtain it. I don't push or pursue until He leads, speaks, or highlights something for me to do. Bill Johnson talks about how when praying for healing or a miracle, we often pray right past it. Meaning, we talk too much instead of speaking or declaring it and trusting in His ability to do the rest. Most of my prayer life revolves around what I call processing with the Father. When something fresh starts coming out of me, I'll write it down or record a voice memo so I can go back and listen for more direction. Then, I'll start declaring it only when He shows me more. Remember, your process and how you talk to the Father will probably be different than mine, but I urge you to push into your relationship with the Father to figure it out if you have not already done so.

The answers to the world around you are already inside of you because He is there. My admonition as I finish this chapter is to challenge you to search out the scriptures for yourself to understand the promises and inherence that already belong to you in the finished work. I recommend that you read E.W. Kenyon's book *Identification: Romance to Redemption* to help you understand the promises and inheritance that are already provided for you. Start going after Father's heart to find out how to manifest His promises for you in your realm of influence. The answers lie in uncovering His promises for you in each season of life that naturally connect with your unique DNA from Him.

Then begin walking out what He highlights in that season. As you do, answers will begin to come from everywhere, not just for you, but also for others around you. We will not only transform culture, but give the Father glory when we start getting answers for ourselves as His children and giving His life away through the answers we bring to those around us. Do you realize it brings the Father glory to give you answers? John 14:13 says, "And whatsoever ye shall ask in my name, that will I do, that the Father may be glorified in the Son." I can tell you that the Father loves to answer questions! If you are a parent, don't you long to give answers for whatever your children might need at their different ages? Matthew 7:11 says, "If you then being evil know how to give good gifts to your children, how much more will your Father who is in heaven give good things to those who ask Him?" The world is looking for you to unpack some of His answers that they can't get from anywhere but Him. So, start unpacking what He highlights in you, and it will be not only what you need and want, but what those around you need and want as well.

You have access to the vault of the Kingdom. You have the keys. Go get the answers for our world and the people around you so they may have their own encounter with the Father. Don't wait. Go at once. Bill Johnson makes this statement, and it is so good. He says, "I'm not sure how to do it, but I'm doing my best to apply it to my life. We owe the world an encounter with the Father." My admonition to you is to find out who you are in Him and what the finished work has provided, and then go give the people in your world an encounter with the Father.

Chapter 3:

THE BLUEPRINT—CONNECTING YOU TO YOUR DESTINY

What are your dreams, desires, and ultimate destiny? What if the Father already placed all the things inside of you that would make you happy and provide a full life? Could it be that all you need is inside of you now? What if your identity is inside you and your prophetic potential already exists within you? What if your potential is tied to you uncovering the gold that the Father has already put in you? Part of your destiny is uncovering and working out the mystery of what the Father has put in your heart. You will be the most fulfilled when you are on the quest of discovering who and what He made you to be. It's an ever-unfolding journey, and if we go with Him on the journey, He will bring us to our greatest potential in life.

In the movie *Transformers*, we see a pioneer named Witwicky with a discovery team searching for something in Antarctica. Witwicky accidentally falls into a 15-foot hole in the snow. The others panic and start to call out to him. Witwicky looks up and knows he has discovered something but doesn't know what. He touches the unknown object and a bright light blasts out, knocks him down, and leaves an imprint of the map to the AllSpark on his glasses. We learn that the map would save humanity one day. Two generations later, Witwicky's grandson finds the glasses and the movie takes off from there.

The AllSpark was a tool designed to save humanity, but if possessed by evil, it would be a tool to destroy it. The good side wanted the AllSpark to help save their system, as well as earth, but there was an evil side looking to use it to destroy the world. What if the real "AllSpark" that is going to save humanity is tied to your destiny and uncovering what is in you? What if your AllSpark has the answers for yourself and humanity around you? Your AllSpark is in your heart. It will not come out of your heart by itself—you must dig it out of your heart and steward it well for it to become a reality in your life.

In Psalms 139:14-16, David talks about how God formed you, and that first and foremost, you are fearfully and wonderfully made. You were skillfully wrought in your mother's womb. His eyes were on you when you were yet unformed. This scripture also reveals something that is often overlooked but is the main thrust of where the core of the story really begins. He mentions the "substance in us," which is actually the DNA of the Father Himself that was put in us before we were ever born. The Father's DNA is tied directly to your destiny, dreams and desires.

When your destiny unfolds from your heart like it is supposed to, it has an innate power to speak to and solve some of the world's problems. What if the blueprint and the map to save humanity and solve the world's problems is imprinted in part on your heart? What if the reason the Lord hasn't come back is that He is waiting for you to save the world systems? Psalms 139:14-16 gives us a glimpse of where and how the Father hid our destiny: it is in the substance that He put in us while we were being formed. When we were born, we came pre-packed with DNA that came from the Father and it comes with a natural bend towards certain things. You were born with natural abilities and innate things that are unique to you. You are naturally drawn to certain things. I call it your dominant neurological agenda (after hearing a speaker make that statement in 2006).

You have an agenda from the Father inside of you. It's wired in you neurologically through your whole system. It's dominant in your life. It is part of your destiny and is aligned with His desire to manifest answers to the world through you. Proverbs 22:6 mentions training children in the way that they should go. The word train in this context means to bend. You should never try to teach or bend a child against their natural bend. This is also true with you. There are certain things that you have a bend toward, and when you identify them, you will start seeing the design God has for you. You come pre-designed, predestined to do what you're called to do.

The Nature of Calling, Desire, and Destiny

You have multiple layers of callings and destinies. Many people feel like they are called to do one thing, and when that one thing isn't working, they are miserable. I've realized that I have multiple things for which I have a calling and destiny. It could even be five to eight things. At any given moment, one or two of them might not be working well, so if you only have one, you're going to be miserable.

I will use David as an example. David was a King. The Word of God says he was a prophet. He was a warrior. He was a husband. He was a songwriter who wrote the Psalms. He was a musician. He was a father. He was a son. These were all part of his identity.

He was also a farmer. This was recorded when we first find him tending to the sheep on his dad's farm. What if David had restricted himself to being a farmer? Don't limit your life's calling to one thing. If you do, you'll be frustrated.

We see in Hebrews 11:1-3 that He starts to give us even more insight about how to unpack our destiny. This word is directly correlated to your blueprint. You can translate the word "substance" as "blueprint." You access the blueprint in your heart through faith. Faith releases you to discover your dreams and desires that are ultimately tied to your destiny.

> *Now faith is the substance of things hoped for,*
> *the evidence of things not seen. For by it the*
> *elders obtained a good report. Through faith we*
> *understand that the worlds were framed by the*
> *word of God, so that things which are seen*
> *were not made of things which do appear.*
> – Hebrews 11:1-3

Faith is birthed out of desire. I am referring to the desire from the Father, not desire that violates the Kingdom's values. If it violates the Kingdom's values, it comes from the wrong father. When it is in line with the Father and the written word and it's in your heart, then it's directly correlated to the substance that's in you. If it's in your heart, you are free to go after it if it lines up with the things you find in the substance, and if it doesn't violate the Father's values. Mark 11:23-24 says "whatsoever you desire when you pray, believe that you receive them, and you shall have them."

You are invited to live your dreams through a journey with the Father as He begins to unfold your destiny. Dreams are your invitation into relationship with the Father. Psalm 37:4 gives us insight when it says that if we delight ourselves in the Lord, He will give us the desires of our heart. When you make Him your delight, He will help you unpack the desires that He put inside of you. As stated earlier, you are prewired for certain things, and as you discover the gold in your substance and unpack the things in your heart, you should only steward the dreams that live inside of you and never look for things outside of you.

What He put in you is tied to your destiny and your authenticity. You will be happiest when you are discovering and unpacking the dreams that resonate with your own heart that cause you to come alive inside and out. This is the divine privilege of being a son and daughter of God—partnering with Him to bring Him glory. The Father gets glory when you experience answered prayers. It brings Him glory when you are one with Him, manifesting the things He put inside of you. The Father loves seeing your joy when the things He put inside of you come out, just like you love seeing the joy in your children when they live out their dreams. Just as you light up when your children discover something in themselves that you knew was already in them, Father God lights up when we discover what He put in us.

John 14:13-14 and John 15:7-8 give us a great explanation and glimpse into the pleasure that the Father takes in our dreams and desires. It really opens up what He thinks about our dreams and going after things in our life. Proverbs 13:12 shows us that dreams tasted by us are like eating and experiencing the tree of life. What if exploring and uncovering the things in you begins to release the tree of life through you? As this happens, the world gets to see and experience the tree of life because you have discovered the gold that God placed inside of you. The very life that you experience when you possess on the outside what was imprinted on the blueprint inside of you is the Father's best. Your Father's best—your dreams and desires showing up—causes you to become more alive. Out of that life comes the tree of life inside of you. People taste it and experience the Father for themselves. Psalms 34:8 says, "Taste and see that the Lord is good."

Part of "tasting" comes through us recognizing and allowing the substance the Father put in us to come alive through us so that the world can see Him. People are naturally attracted to people who are fully alive and have something coming through them that brings fulfillment in life. The branches of the tree of life grow through us as we experience desire realized. Desire produces not only life through us, but also gives shade for others to run under and feel the very nature of the Father. Proverbs 13:12 is clear:

> *Hope deferred maketh the heart sick: but when the desire cometh, it is a tree of life.*

Desire realized is the tree of life. Then it says, "hope deferred makes the heart grow sick."

Unfulfilled dreams can kill your heart, so the Father Himself invites you into a journey of discovering what's inside of you. Jesus makes statements like: "Whatever you ask the Father in my name, I will do it" (see John 14:13) and "Whatever you desire when you pray, believe that you have it and you'll receive it" (see Mark 11:23-24). John 15:7-8 says when we get our desires by asking and seeing what is in us, it brings Him glory.

One of the first century saints, Saint Irenaeus of Lyons, said, "The glory of God is man fully alive." I was taught growing up in church that I had a cross to bear, which implied that it would be painful most of the time, and that I must die to everything that brings life to me; apparently, it was bad for me to enjoy life. I believed that if everything was going well for me, I wasn't following the Lord. I thought that the Father would send me on a mission to a country where I didn't want to go to. I was also taught that if I have too much wealth, I might be deceived and not get into heaven. I needed to make sure that I fasted and prayed enough, prayed in tongues all the time, and read the Word all the time so that I would become a real disciple.

I thought that in all my extra time, I should serve and volunteer in church, and if I tried hard enough, I may find favor and acceptance by the Father. I thought that if I proved to Him that I was willing to crawl across broken glass to do His will, and I proved to Him my worth, then I would finally be accepted. I believed this for the first 20 years of my Christian walk after I had recommitted my life to the Lord when I was 20 years old.

Breakdown or Breakthrough?

In 2004, I had a spiritual meltdown that pretty much broke me inside. I didn't know what to believe anymore. I began to ask different questions and have different thoughts, and through it, some of the greatest things started happening. I found myself broken by the very thing that was supposed to give me life—church (or religion). I began to search, and I discovered one foundational scripture that started to change me: Matthew 7:11 which said that if human fathers that are evil know how to give good things to their children and do right by them, then how much more will your Father in heaven give to those who ask?

I realized that I believed that I would do more for my children than the Father would do for me. I was treating God like He was evil. Well-meaning believers presented the Father in such an abusive way that if I treated my children like that, I would have been jailed for child abuse. This passage burned in me for a year and four months. I still felt abused and confused about who He really was. I felt abandoned and broken, but I knew I couldn't live like that anymore—crawling over broken glass trying to prove my worth to Him. I wasn't going to raise my children like that either.

At that time, God introduced me to a few new mentors, and I began to change my standards and beliefs. They helped me see the world differently, and I started changing from the inside out. It began as just new information. I still wasn't sure how to walk that out. Then, in 2006, I had an encounter with the Father Himself that forever changed and marked my life. I won't take time to tell all that happened because it would take an entire book, but I will give some highlights. I truly believe I met the Father Himself for the first time. He asked me a question one day that reiterated a promise I had heard 20 years earlier about some things He was going to do in our city. At that point, God and I weren't on speaking terms, except for me blaming Him for the abuse I had experienced in the church at the hands of the leaders who were supposed to be protecting me.

My response to Him at that time was, "Don't talk to me about that. You need to talk to that pastor on the stage. I'm not interested." I even said it out loud. What He said began to burn in me, and I couldn't get away from it. About two weeks later, He said, "Tell your wife." My response was, "I'm not going to tell her. She is still hurt, broken, and depressed from what happened. YOU tell her." He did. I came home a few days later and she looked different. She was journaling and she told me, "You won't believe what the Father said." After that, for a solid year, it felt like God had moved into our home. Everywhere we went, I would have random encounters that I couldn't explain.

I'd be driving 70 mph on the highway and I would have to pull over because the presence was so overwhelming I couldn't drive. Encounters would happen in the shower. The shower became our holy of holies it seemed—it was so normal for Him to wreck me there, in a good way. Many times, I would be on the floor; I couldn't stand. I couldn't stop crying because of the joy and love I was feeling. During that time, God started revealing how good He actually is. About halfway through that year, He spoke to me and said, "I'm going to break all of your rules about me." He did.

These rules were not against the Word of God, but the interpretation and the beliefs that I had developed around doctrinal thought. I thought I was right and that my theology was completely correct. He kindly corrected my incorrect beliefs about Him. Through a year of encounters and revealing my call, His love, and how good He really was, my wife and I were transformed into different people—finally into sons and daughters of the Father. Our lives have not been the same since. The Father is a genius. He's not going to work or lead you against the way He made you and the substance He placed in you. There are things hidden in your heart that He hasn't uncovered yet. He started uncovering those things in me in 2006. My wife and I had been walking with the Lord for 25 years and there were things in my heart that He had not yet revealed. Sometimes it's about the right timing and our growth before He can show us some of those things that are hidden in our substance. Our part in the revealing process is to go after what He reveals and to steward it well until He reveals the next thing from our blueprint. As Martin Luther King Jr. said, "You don't have to see the whole staircase, just take the first step."

The Delight of the Father

The Father delights to see your answered prayer. He delights to see your desires come to fruition. He delights in seeing you being one with Him and seeing His plan that He placed inside of you come to pass. He walks with you in the process. We try to create systems, principles, and destiny from things on the outside of us. I did this for years. We usually grab for the things outside of us because that's where we find our first information. I began to find out that as we create these systems and principles to find things on the outside of us, it has to line up to the pre-packed thing on the inside of us. You were pre-charged with power, destiny, and blueprints inside of you to manifest His will through you.

Your desires and dreams have eternal impact on people around you, cities, and nations. The Word tells us that "desire realized is like the tree of life." As these desires come through you, it will cause people to eat of the tree of life. The tree of life was in the garden. When Adam and Eve were put out of the garden, they couldn't eat of the tree of life anymore. According to Proverbs 13:12, when desire is realized, it is the tree of life. When you are born again, and as you find the substance of the tree of life within you, you become a new creature. The new creature inside of you begins to grow and as your natural desires begin to come to pass, people can see, taste, and find the Lord.

You now have become the temple of God, so the tree of life that was in the garden is now in you. The Father is in you according to Jesus. You are one with the Father and Him according to His prayer in John 17:22. When we manifest our desires, people taste them, and they are eternally imprinted and impacted in their souls and they have a choice to see the Father themselves. Your dreams and desires were designed to eternally impact lives now on this earth and in this time.

> *And the glory which thou gavest me I have given*
> *them; that they may be one, even as we are one:*
> – John 17:22

What if the world is crying out for certain things on the tree of life, and that certain part is hidden inside of you? The world wants the Father and Jesus, but many times they aren't seeing a picture of Him through us that is compelling, and they don't know how wonderful He is. I've realized that certain things have come through me to people in the world, and it reflected and produced His image on them. Then, those people had a choice to make because they saw the Father and the Son through me, and they could either choose Him or not.

What if that which the world is crying out for on the tree of life is hidden within you, and the world is waiting for you to uncover it so that they can experience the answers from the Father Himself and for themselves? What if we as the body of Christ have parts of His intentionality of what the Father wants the world systems and the spheres to be like?

God is interested in answering people's questions. When your desires come out of the substance He placed inside of you, they result in answers to someone's question. Unfortunately, the church has tried to answer questions that the world is not asking. What if we, through the blueprints He put inside of us as individuals and as a corporate body of believers, began to answer the questions the world is asking because of what was coming through us naturally? Through the journey of discovering what the Father put in you and bringing it out, it shows His intentions for the world and how good He really is.

Discovering these things in you will allow you to have influence and rise to help rescue the systems and disciple nations. You were built to answer the world's problems. What if through realizing your desires, the world sees how good the Father is and that He is in a good mood and loves them? In my different experiences in the companies I have helped to start or co-found, following the highlights and desires that started bubbling up in my heart, I wasn't always sure in the moment if it was the right direction to go at certain crossroads. As I grew over time, I developed a practice that helped me at least explore the desire. If what was being highlighted didn't violate anything in the scriptures or the values of the Kingdom, then I knew I could explore it to see if it was the right direction to go. You must learn to gain answers in smaller matters if you expect God to give you larger ones to solve. Luke 16:10 (NLT version) says that if you are faithful in little things, you will be faithful in large ones. This is how the Kingdom works.

I will share a story that will help you see how answers can come through desires or highlights that the Father brings through your heart in a particular season. In the spring of 1998, I was trying to decide if I should expand the company I was leading at the time, and I met a gentleman at a larger company in the same industry. We did some business together and that led to a suggestion from him that I start a new service within the business my father and I had at the time. It seemed like the right thing to do, so we started building it and by 2001, we had built another multi-million-dollar business within our current company and then sold it.

We then started building this same service again in 2002, and when the economy collapsed at the end of 2008, the only reason we didn't go under like many of our competitors was because of the desire I had and the answer that came during that season. Because of that service, we were able to stay in the game until the economy rebounded. This is just one example for us to realize the power of answers through our desires that He gives us, that will not only save businesses but also save our Nation and the systems that the Father loves. John 3:16-17 says that God so loved the world that He gave His son—He so loved the systems that He put in place. What if through your desires and dreams coming to pass, He wants to heal the systems? What if through us rising up in this way and serving through influence and leadership and answering people's problems we could ascend and take control of the systems as He intended?

When I say control, I mean in a sense of displacing darkness and making sure light is at the top of the systems that will reflect the image of how He created them. As a result, His thoughts and ways would dominate the systems instead of the enemies. You would begin to rise and have influence as sons in the Father's business finding His will for others again and releasing His glory through them.

DREAMS

To help describe the word "dream" and the steps needed to accomplish your dreams, I created the following acronym:

D – Desire of the Father.
R– Realizing the dreams in your heart.
E – Experiencing your capacity to grow into your dreams.
A – Adaptability and pruning that comes with growth.
M – Mastery of your gifts, talents, and abilities.

Repeat these steps as you advance toward your dreams. As one dream is obtained, you head off to a new dream and the process of you growing up to be able to realize another dream will take place. You will notice that adaptability and pruning is required to accomplish your dreams. One of my mentors says that the reason God prunes you is to keep you from being killed when he pours out His blessing upon you. In other words, the blessing is so huge that if we're not pruned, it may destroy us. The pruning process in our lives isn't meant to be painful or prolonged, but is necessary to bring forth new blooms and dreams in our life.

If you don't trim back and prune your plants when it's time, they won't produce the blooms and strong stems needed to keep them from breaking under the pressure that comes in the different seasons. Every good and perfect gift comes from the Father, and He wouldn't be a good Father if He didn't take you through processes that will inspire personal growth so that you are ready for where He is taking you next—which is always to dig more of the treasure out that He put inside of you before you were born. So, allow the vinedresser to do His job when it's necessary. Pruning of a plant strengthens the plant and allows it to produce better fruit. That is what the pruning of the Lord does to us as we pursue the dreams He has placed in our hearts; we become stronger and can continue to grow into all He has called us to be.

Your Big Yes

What is the big YES in you? What if experiencing your big YES actually shows the world who He is? I call it a divine manifest obsession. The substance in you begins to burn and as you unpack it and find the blueprint in you, it becomes an obsession. I know you may be thinking, "I don't need to have an obsession." It's a divine manifest obsession—something that burns in you that you can't get away from. It's wonderful, not bad. What if that thing you can't escape from brings presence, power, glory, wisdom, and answers through it for the world and yourself? What if intimacy with the Father births something in us and through us of the Kingdom?

The art of achievement and personal transformation is in walking with the Father and manifesting your desires. Surrender to the desire of the Father—all of Him covering all of you. The glory of God being man fully alive. What if you being fully alive with what burns in you and the desires coming out of you reveal the glory of God to the world? Your potential lies in the thought that you will walk out through life's process and unpack the treasure that the Father put in you. As you see more of the pieces of that blueprint, He will start bringing a compelling future out of you. Not only for you, but those around you. It's a discovery of personal purpose and destiny that comes from strategic interventions from Him. Discovering the dreams He placed in you is an invitation into intimacy. Your dreams have eternal impact. It takes divine direction to steward your dreams because some of them are really big.

To find pieces of the blueprint in you, ask yourself these questions:

- What makes you happy?
- What makes you smile?
- What makes you feel a sense of accomplishment?
- What turns you on and lights you up?
- What fills your soul?
- What feeds you?
- What makes you feel free?
- What makes you feel frustrated and mad?
- What challenges you because you see pain and you want to fix it?

These are indicators that help reveal what already exists inside you. There's a Kingdom created around this tree of life—a value already put in you before you were ever born.

How do we know if our dreams are of God? We should know by the values of the King. If anything within us violates His values and the Word, they are not of Him. It's a quick test to see if you should consider pursuing a dream. If a dream contradicts the Word and the Kingdom's values, it's not of Him.

Here are indicators that the dreams coming out of you are from Him:

- Are the people around you and under your leadership being transformed?
- Does your dream open up a place for others to grow and be promoted?
- Is it bringing wholeness and wellness and healthy growth?
- Does your ceiling become a floor for others from which they can accomplish even more than you?
- Do people step up into a higher place because of your dreams? If it creates a stepping stone and part of history that has eternal impact, then it's probably the Father.

God had a dream, and he wrapped your body around it and sent you to planet earth.

With His substance in you, He wants to manifest His dream, destiny, and desire through you. He has given you all the tools you will ever need. Everything you need is in you now. Once the new creature is formed inside of you, as Paul said, there is a forming that takes place over time, and the hidden things within you will begin to bubble up and manifest through you. Those things coming up within you are invitations from the Father. We should listen to these things as we work out our own walk with Him.

What dreams did God wrap you in and send you to earth for? The manifestation of those will produce the tree of life for the world and solve problems in our cities. We will become a light and a river of living water in the streets of our cities and begin to heal our land and destroy evil. When we start unraveling and unpacking what was put in us by Him, it releases life everywhere. Let us be a people who unpacks the blueprint of Him in us and allows Him to impact nations through us.

Chapter 4

IDENTITY CRISIS

We have forgotten who we are as sons and daughters of God. We have forgotten that He left us in charge of His creation and that we are called a holy nation as believers. What we do within our nations should have a national impact. If we were to remember who we are as sons and daughters, would we move and govern as the Father intended? In most cases, we have reduced the call we have as governing saints and the greatest story ever told down to Sunday church, and a feel-good community that's built on comfort and convenience for you and me. We come together and put on our best before each other. "I'm fine. You're fine. I have my family, my cars, my life, my home, and you have yours."

We have built a feel-good false grace and wealth culture in the western church that causes us to measure success by how many people gather on Sunday, how big our buildings are, how well our people are doing, or how well our missions are doing overseas. We continue to measure the success of the church by how many people we are able to help who are in need. The Father's primary measurement begins with nations being discipled and then the other things follow. We have lost most of our impact and national influence on the moral character of our nations. In the western world, the cultural war for our nations has been won and dominated by people whose agenda is different than the Father's.

It's important to save others and care for the less fortunate—these are Biblical mandates. We should do both, and point people to what Jesus has done for them. This is paramount, and it is the first step to access the inheritance for which Jesus paid. Most churches have majored in preaching the gospel of salvation and helping others in need, but there is so much more when we remember that we are sons and daughters of the Father.

Wealth and Blessing

According to the Word of God, Jesus ratified the Abrahamic covenant for us, including the blessings of Abraham. We are not only the sons of the Father, we are also the sons of Abraham according to Galatians 3:7-14. The covenant the Father made with Abraham is our inheritance as well. This includes having or creating wealth and abundance in every way in our lives for advancing the Kingdom (Deuteronomy 8:18). As we advance His Kingdom, the Lord also wants us to have some personal enjoyment along the way. I love what one of my mentors, Bill Johnson, says about this—that it's impossible for the hose that's dispersing the water not to get wet while the water flows through it. We are called to be the hoses of blessing of the Kingdom. The Father said that all nations would be blessed through the seeds (generations) of Abraham.

The Father wants us to be blessed to the capacity of our dreams. We must be able to gain wealth, influence, favor, and power, which are all types of currency in the world (money, fame, influence, power), without our hearts being lifted beyond our capacity and ability (see Ezekiel 28:1-3) and letting it go to our ego. Will we trust Him instead of the wealth? Will you trust the wealth you created vs. trusting the Father who gave you the power to create wealth (see Mark 10:24)?

Ezekiel 28:1-3 is a warning to protect us from our hearts being lifted above our capacity from the Creator. Mark 10:24 reminds us that we shouldn't trust in what we have instead of the Father. In Romans 1:25, Paul makes a statement that the Roman worshipped and served the creation instead of the Creator. When everything we touch begins to prosper and all our dreams come to pass, will we keep our hearts connected to the Father as the giver of all good things, or will we forget Him? Deuteronomy 8:18 says that He has given us the power to get wealth. The moment we take Him out of the equation, we are saying that we trust the wealth more than Him.

We have reduced wealth and inheritance to just cash-in-hand or the things we can purchase with the cash. This is a very narrow view. I'm for abundance for all of God's people, but it was never intended only for you. We are called to allow our wealth to flow from us into avenues to advance the Kingdom. We are not supposed to create a "bless me" club or a feel-good community of saints that don't know how to advance His agenda through Kingdom thought and culture.

In the United States and the west, we have in most cases reduced grace to be only for ourselves and our family's empowerment to have a good life on earth. Grace was given to us to develop Kingdom cultural reformers and transformers of nations. The Father enjoys His children being blessed with all good things, but to whom much is given, much is required. In 1 Corinthians 15:10, Paul states, "I am what I am by the grace of God." He then says that he has worked harder than all the others (meaning the other Apostles), but immediately after that statement, he says, "Yet, not I, but the grace of God that was with me." This insight shows us how powerful grace really is. It is much more than a Band-Aid for our weakness and sins, which is how it has been treated in our nation. Based on this scripture, it is the very power of God that rests on us and works through us to advance the Kingdom. The grace of God will overwhelm and remove the challenges that come against us as we advance on our mission to accomplish His agenda.

One of the questions we must answer is, "Who did He leave in charge?" According to the Word of God, He left *us* in charge. We haven't taken that seriously. Genesis 1:28-29 tells us that Adam and Eve were supposed to go, subdue, take dominion, and multiply and be fruitful. Through this very first mandate of God, He gives us access to His power and authority to rule and serve all places in His earth that

He created. Obviously, the fall hindered that process when Adam and Eve decided they knew best, but the good news is that the last Adam, Jesus Christ, redeemed all that was lost and gave us the keys of the Kingdom to advance His Kingdom and His ways once again. He never intended for us to be without His presence or answers for life. The world is looking for you to manifest His word and the answers that come through advancing His Kingdom.

Our Greatest Issue is Our Weakened Identity

This weakening of our identity has happened gradually over the last 100 years. Until we begin to see ourselves as the Father sees us, we will not be strong enough to disciple the nations. We must once again realize that we are sons and daughters of the Father given the mission to advance His business and His agenda. We must start seeing ourselves as heirs of our Father and joint heirs with Jesus (Romans 8:17). When you are a joint heir in our governing law in America, you are equal with that other person—on the same level. We need to restore what Jesus paid for, our true identity as sons and daughters of the Father who have access to everything that flows from the Father.

It was said of the early apostolic movement in Acts 17:5-6 that those who turned the last city upside down are now on their way to their city. When you read the entire chapter, you will realize this wasn't a positive endorsement of the apostles. The next city on the path of the apostles was not rolling out the welcome mat as they came to town. Wherever the early apostles went, they caused disruption to the status quo in the culture. The power and authority they walked in resulted in that disruption. The power and authority on them contested every spirit that wasn't of God. As a result, it contested those to whom the spirits were attached or operating through. It caused friction to entire cities, but through the power of the Father in the apostles, whole cities were won. They changed and shifted the original culture in cities into a Kingdom culture.

Isaiah 2:2-3 says that in the last days, the mountain of the Lord's house will be at the top of the mountain over every nation. In the Lord's Prayer, it states to pray this way, "...Your will be done on earth as it is in heaven" (see Matthew 6:10), meaning that we should be drawing heaven down to earth. Kingdom culture can overtake an ungodly culture when the prevailing spirit or attitude over a community, state, or nation is that of the Holy Spirit. How we do life as people flows from His value system to all people in our nation regardless of their particular belief. Proverbs 29:2 says, "When the righteous are in authority, the people rejoice; But when a wicked man rule, the people groan." This verse highlights that a prevailing spirit of righteousness impacts all those under the realm of that spirit.

One of our greatest concerns as believers is that we don't want any friction in our lives. We are not used to conflict, and will do everything we can to avoid it, even in the face of things that are contrary to our beliefs and what the Word teaches. We avoid hard questions and anything that appears as if we are trying to correct or disciple someone. We don't want to address anything we see that is wrong in our communities, often in the name of 'love.' We have partnered with the religious spirit, the politically correct spirit, and the traditions of men. We have backed away from providing Godly input for the way our cities and nations should be governed. We have bowed before the spirit of the world and have allowed the leaven of the Kingdom to lay waste in us. Let's explore our true identity and how to restore it, so we will give Jesus His reward of people and nations.

Understanding Your True Identity

In Philippians 2:8, Jesus said that He didn't think it was robbery to be made equal with God, but humbled Himself to the death of the cross. In John 10:30-34, Jesus has a teaching moment with the Pharisees as He unfolds who He is, the Son of God, but they could not hear or see it. The Pharisees pick up rocks to stone Him as He continues to reveal His true identity. He stopped them and asked them, "For which of the miracles are you going to stone me?" And they replied, "For none of them, but for your blasphemy because you being a man make yourself God." Jesus' next statement is telling, and something we have to look into for ourselves. He says to them, "Does not your law say that you are gods?" Jesus was referencing Psalms 82:6, which says, "I said, You are gods, and all of you are children of the Most High." The Pharisees realized that He had quoted the scriptures correctly, and they dropped their rocks.

In our culture, we don't necessarily relate to what was being said in those statements. But in the Jewish culture of that day, once a son became of age, he was given a party that said to everyone in the Jewish community that now as a son he could speak for his father. The son was given a ring and a family robe that signified that he was equal with the father in word and deed. The son was then considered equal in his father's business and in the marketplace. Whatever the son said was backed by his father. If the son bought something, it was the same as his father buying it. If the son gave his word to someone, it was the same as the father's word. Any commitment that the son made, the father made as well and had to honor it. When Jesus said, "I'm the Son of God," it made Him equal with the Father in the eyes of the Pharisees because of what the law and their practiced culture dictated. They went a little crazy because they couldn't believe He would say that.

Hence, in the gospels that follow, every time He refers to Himself as the Son in front of the religious leaders, they tried to kill him. Why? Because in doing so, He made himself equal with the Father. Stay with me as we unpack the insights in this chapter and look to the scriptures and references that I'll be giving you. Don't be quick to dismiss what you are reading because it doesn't necessarily fit into your current beliefs. Be open to hear and see. I love what Bill Johnson says, "God will sometimes offend your mind to reveal what's in your heart."

In John 17:22, Jesus made us one with the Father through His finished work on the cross. The interesting thing about this is that it puts us on the same level as Jesus, and if that's true, then suddenly we find ourselves one with the Father as well. Now I do understand that it's only through His finished work that this is possible, and not in our own power. While this stretches many of us, we must begin to get back to our true identity, the way He sees us, in order to become champions who can rescue systems from the clutches of evil. In Romans 8:17 and Ephesians 2:6-10, Paul says we are heirs and joint heirs, meaning 'same.' He says we have been seated with Him in heavenly places. It's interesting that God made Adam and Eve in His image and likeness because He wanted people like Him to fellowship with as family.

After studying and experiencing personal encounters and revelation on this subject from the Lord, I am of the persuasion that the Father wanted to create someone like Him with whom He could walk, build life, and be family. In other words, He wanted to create an equal in His likeness with whom to do life. I know when I use the word equal and likeness, bells start sounding off, but again I want you to understand that if you were a son in the Jewish culture at that time, you became equal with the father of that house. So, the whole purpose for us is that the Father wanted a family of sons and daughters that could rule and reign *with* Him here in the world and the one to come. If the word equal distresses you, then just start realizing and adopting that you are a son or daughter of the King, and that you are royalty in this life and the one to come. With Him, we can change culture and transform our world into one, which brings Him glory.

Until we start believing in who we are, we won't complete His mandate. As long as we think He's wonderful and we're not, as long as we think He can do anything but we can't, as long as we diminish our role in history and our identity of being one with the Father, we will never contest and contend for the systems of nations because of what we think about ourselves. What we think about God is the most important thing about us. But what God thinks about us will transform us into champions able to do great things with the Father in the Kingdom.

We will never find the Father's best for us if we think He alone solely controls our destiny, or believe we have no say in it, or think to ourselves, "It must be His will that the world is getting worse." If we buy into incomplete truths like this and never explore our sonship and what true sonship means, we will never find the Father's best for us. Our destiny is up to us, at least in part. Remember the parable of the talents? If you don't exercise your talents, you won't go where He intended. It's up to you. Maybe the world is getting worse because the people He left in charge have given it over to the world system to run everything, since our identity is so weak. Maybe we don't think we can lead in the world or that we are to go into the world because the world might influence us. Being one with the Father doesn't remove your responsibility to do your part. We are called to go into the world, like Jesus, and take action for what the Father is calling us to do.

Authority, Inheritance, and Responsibility

Let me give you a few scriptures that show what He thinks about your authority, inheritance, and responsibility to execute.

John 14:13 – "And whatever you ask in My name, that I will do, that the Father may be glorified in the Son."

Matthew 18:18 – "Assuredly, I say to you, whatever you bind on earth will be bound in heaven, and whatever you loose on earth will be loosed in heaven."

John 20:23 – "If you forgive the sins of any, they are forgiven them; if you retain the sins of any, they are retained"

Matthew 10:8 – "Heal the sick, cleanse the lepers, raise the dead, cast out demons. Freely you have received, freely give."

He didn't say, "Pray for these things to happen." He said, "Go and do it." Not only did He leave us in charge, but He gave us commands, promises, and mandates on how to rule. It sounds like He has given us his signet ring and whatever we say goes. Whatever you ask in the Father's name is to come forth.

Job 22:28 – "You will also declare a thing, and it will be established for you."

Beliefs and Experiences

One reason we don't operate as He commanded is because we allow our beliefs and theology to be based upon what someone has said or taught us instead of what the Father said. Another reason is because many well-meaning Christians don't believe that the Word of God means what it says. We paraphrase or translate the Word to the point we miss the real meaning of what He said. In the process, we lose our identity, as we are not taught who we really are and what belongs to us. Therefore, as a free people, we need to study the Word for ourselves and have our own encounters with the Father that should lead us to practical application of the insight or revelation from the Father.

We should then have our own experiences, and through them our beliefs become a working part of our lives that produce fruit and reveal the Kingdom and the heart of the Father for us and the people around us. Until our beliefs align with the truth of who He really created us to be, we really don't have an anointing to impart it to others. The Word says freely we have received and freely we give it away (see Matthew 10:8). If you don't receive it, you can't give it. If you don't believe it, you can't receive it.

In 1517, Martin Luther nailed his thesis to the door of the Catholic Church, and there was a declaration made in the realm of the spirit that day that would change church culture forever. There are 95 points in his thesis. Two of the primary shifts and outgrowths of his thesis were that the just should live by faith, and that the Pope and the ministers could not sell indulgences that replaced true repentance. The main declaration that was made was one of freedom in Christ and that we have direct access to Christ instead of having a man serve as a mediator between us and God. This shift in thought started the Protestant movement, and I believe it helped inspire the birth of America. The great-grandparents of our Founding Fathers were alive at that time and heard the stories of freedom in Christ. I believe they started dreaming of a land where they could worship freely and unencumbered by the control of state religion. It was one of the powerful reasons that they came to America to establish a land where their children could be free. Like Martin Luther, one person can change history with the right identity. That person can be you when you realize that you are one with the Father.

We are who He says we are based on the finished work of Jesus. He has empowered us and placed so much confidence in us that in Matthew 10:11-15, He talks about the disciples going into cities to find a house that was worthy for them to stay. It's an interesting thought that He said, "worthy for you to stay." If the home received them, they were to leave their peace. If the home did not receive them, they were to take their peace back. Jesus went on to say that if the city did not receive them or their words, it would be worse for them than Sodom and Gomorrah on the day of judgment. That is how much confidence Jesus has in His disciples, including you and me. That's a pretty big thought because Sodom and Gomorrah were two of the most sinful places on earth—because these cities rejected the sons and daughters of God, they will be judged even more harshly. To be clear, my point is not about judgment and sin, but the power and authority He expects us to walk in. He expects us to go rescue and restore the world around us as sons and daughters of the King.

Until we completely believe this, we won't be able to carry the weight of our assignment to represent the Kingdom on earth and help accomplish all the Father has promised the world. He's a good Father, and He will only give us what we can carry and won't destroy us. We are His bride, and He is waiting for the bride to grow up into her potential so He can release everything that she needs to rule and serve the world. Jesus paid the ultimate price to empower us to reclaim the current systems of this world and bring them back to what He intended them to be. If we don't reestablish our identity, we will not accomplish our mission.

We must start acting like Kings, priests, sons, daughters, and ambassadors in Christ. We must believe we are the head and not the tail (Deuteronomy 28:13), and that we are called to lead, influence, serve, and govern our world in the same way as if the Father were here doing it Himself. When we operate in who we were made to be, we will have answers for the world's problems. The world is crying out for answers, but we want be able to access them until we gain a greater picture of our identity.

When we lose our identity, all other losses are automatic. It's only a matter of time. When Adam and Eve fell, they lost their identity. Adam lived 900 years, but he lost everything when he lost his identity. It just took time for it to show up. Jesus came, died on the cross, and rose from the dead to restore our identity as sons and daughters of the Father. We've been given the keys, authority and power, and unlimited resources to govern, serve, and rule with His heart and to restore all that was destroyed from the time of Adam to Jesus. It's up to us to rescue and restore humanity and the systems from the clutches of darkness into His glorious light.

I believe God is calling us to rise up as knights, champions in our time, to restore what has been lost. We get a glimpse of what knights of God look like when we look at the description of the mighty men of David (2 Samuel 23:8-

39) and what Joel 2:1-12 describes as people who are great and strong, like people who have never been before. You are a knight. Now is the time in history for the knights to begin to arise and for her majesty, the bride, to take her rightful place on the throne of David—to serve creation and to govern and restore the world with His heart, ways, wisdom, and love.

Gifts and Callings

So much of our theology for Kingdom life is based on waiting on the return of Jesus so we can escape the earth, go to Heaven, and rule and reign with Him forever. If we think that the Father is going to put an untested bride on the throne to rule with His Son, we are wrong. We have been irresponsible in many cases with our development. We have been waiting on the Father and He has been waiting on us to grow up enough to handle what He wants to pour out that will transform the world around us. If we don't develop our potential and the things He placed in us, He won't pour out what's needed to transform our world. A lot of our life is contingent upon us walking out our gifts, talents, and potential that were put in us before we were born (see Psalm 139-14-16).

David talks about this hidden substance placed within us before we were born. The Father put things in you called gifts and callings. He won't take them back. The parable of the talents teaches us that He's counting on us to exercise our gifts and talents. It's interesting in the parable of the talents that the master of the house left the servants immediately, once He gave them the talents. Note that the master did not tell the servants what to do, where to do it, when or how to do it. He gave them their talents, left, and expected them to take action—which doesn't fit most of our theology today. Today, we would have a prayer meeting, wait on the Lord, fast, or teach on being hungrier hoping that He would show up. As you mature and build your relationship with the Father, through experience and encounters, you learn His heart and His ways. You start activating the gifts and talents He put inside of you to bring His Kingdom into your life and the lives of others around you.

Matthew 7:11 says, "If you then, being evil, know how to give good gifts to your children, how much more will your Father who is in heaven give good things to those who ask Him!" In many cases, we treat the Father as if He isn't as good as our natural fathers. As our children mature, we expect them to know the rules and ways we taught them as their parents. We also give them more responsibility when they show us that they can handle it. The Father is much smarter than we are as parents. He gives to us based on our own ability, and expects us to produce a result. Just like we expect our children to grow into responsible adults, and not stay children, the Father expects us to become responsible 'adults' as sons and daughters. Just like we stop doing certain things for our children as they learn to be responsible, He does the same. He expects us to use our gifts and talents to accomplish what He has called us to do.

Once you come into the Kingdom by being born again and filled with the Spirit, everything else is accrued through your belief, trust, and action. He never promises to complete your potential or give you favor, influence, authority, or anointing just because you're born again. I know this statement may bother you, but after your conversion and baptism in the Holy Spirit, most of your life and maturity must be worked out by walking and having intimacy with the Father. Without being responsible for ourselves, and through self-government and awareness through Him teaching us, we will miss most of what He has planned for us.

Life in the Kingdom is about trust and mystery. We have to be responsible to engage with the Holy Spirit to find out the endless possibilities that are available through our relationship with Him. This is not a work-based or rules-based theology, it's about relationship and intimacy with the Father. It's about His grace and empowerment to live this life from the place of relationship. Through our relationship with the Father, we access the Kingdom of heaven and what He has given us by faith and hope in Him. We must begin to believe in ourselves again and start seeing ourselves the way the Father sees us. 2 Corinthians 3:18 reminds us that as we behold His glory, like we are looking in a mirror, we are transformed into the same image from glory to glory, by the Holy Spirit.

We must begin to throw off all the religious ideas that don't save systems of the world and disciple nations. We must rise and start reforming and transforming our world. Romans 8:19 says that creation is waiting for the manifestation of the sons (and daughters) of God. I believe this means creation and the world are waiting for the knights to rise up and take their place as a governing body that will do the right things that the Father needs in order to restore and rescue the world from darkness. Jesus said it is finished. He left us in charge, and He is waiting for us to make it so. He is not sitting in the throne room worried about what will happen. He has full confidence in us when we operate in our true identity. He put everything we will ever need inside of us to do the job He has called us to do. It is in us now, we just need to go do what He said to do. Let's answer creation's call to manifest the Kingdom!

Jesus gave us the keys of the Kingdom to bind (shut up) and loose (open) things on the earth according to His divine order (see Matthew 16:19). In Isaiah 9:6, there's a promise that says the government will rest upon His shoulders. Paul later tells us that we are a part of the Body of Christ and ultimately, He is the head of the body. He is NOT the shoulders—in this dispensation of the Kingdom age, we are (see 1 Corinthians 12:18-26). So, His government rests upon us. We have His delegated authority on earth while He is gone. Just like the three people who received the talents in the parable of the talents, they were to do their best with these and produce what the master wanted. The Father wants us to take our rightful place here to govern with a heart of love, wisdom, and understanding of His ways for humanity and His mind for them. He believes in us much more than we believe in ourselves. It's time for our belief in us to catch up with the Father's.

The world is waiting for the Father, whether they realize it or not, because He is so good that everybody wants a Father like Him. Once they see Him through us, they will see how good He is. We think the world doesn't want the Father.

The reality is that they don't want the Father that is presented to them because of our inability to truly identify as sons and daughters. Jesus told the disciples, "If you have seen Me, you have seen the Father." This may stretch you a bit, but like Jesus, we should be able to say that when you have seen me, you have seen the Father. Jesus said in Matthew 10:40, "He who receives you receives me, and he who receives me receives Him who sent Me." The world can only see the Father when we operate in our identity as His sons and daughters.

When I began to realize my identity as a son, my questions started changing as I searched to know more. I asked myself, "What do I believe and why? What did God really say, and what are man's ideas about what He thought and said?" It's important that in every season of your life that you allow your theology and thoughts about God and His Word to be challenged and sometimes changed into greater revelations because of the encounters you have with the Father and the words of the prophets. This is how the early church in the book of Acts did life. They didn't have the New Testament of the Bible. They had only the prophets, the Old Testament, and what they heard Jesus teach, directly or indirectly by the Holy Spirit. Despite what we would perceive as limitations, they changed the world.

I sometimes wonder if our reliance on the written word of God has, at times, limited our sight for what the living Word, Jesus, and the Father are doing. Do we run the risk of being like the Pharisees? They knew the law, the prophets, and were able to quote the law from memory. But, they missed the person being revealed in Old Testament scripture—Jesus. After 35 years in the church with top leadership roles in two different ministries, I've learned that we tend to form our doctrinal beliefs and thoughts based upon what we were taught when we first started our walk with the Lord. Then we take on the doctrines of the movements we become a part of during our lives. When the Father moves to the next thing, we tend to stay with what worked in the past—safe and certain. The problem is that we may not realize we are living in an old box of the past season.

When the Father moves to the next thing and we are bound and enslaved to that old box, we will fight to the death to keep what He did. It becomes no more than traditions of men with a Bible wrapped around it. I'm not saying that He won't still show up there, but He is limited because of our belief. Because He is good and loves people so much, He will still show up and heal and touch and bring deliverance to people. I've seen it happen. One of the movements I grew up in had miracles, signs, and wonders that as a young believer I assumed were God's approval of the leaders and the movement. I now realize that often the reason He shows up is because of His mercy and love for people, not necessarily because He is validating what we believe. Many times, we accept things into our beliefs that aren't His identity for us. We tend to skip and avoid parts of the Bible we don't understand or that don't fit into our theology.

Wise as Serpents

Mystery is part of the Kingdom and we can't explain everything God does or doesn't do. In Matthew 10:16, Jesus said to "be wise as serpents and harmless as doves." The context for this statement is that Jesus is telling His disciples that they are being sent out as sheep among wolves. I was always told that this scripture meant that the shepherd protected the sheep because they couldn't protect themselves against wolves—sheep have no protection against wolves and are lunch for the wolves. I was taught that Jesus, the Shepherd, can protect you, but that isn't what He said.

In this scripture, Jesus said your protection, directive, direct influence with the world, and success is based on being wise as serpents. Then He said, "beware of men" (Matthew 10:17). Connecting the two thoughts together, Jesus is telling them, and us, that being wise as serpents would be sufficient for your protection from both the world and men. Think about how Jesus says, "I am sending you out as sheep among wolves," then He says, "Beware of men." Why? Because they're going take you before the councils and possibly either throw you in jail or kill you. Here in the middle of you, being eaten or killed is how to engage in the world. "Be wise as serpents and harmless as doves." Everything the Father does is in order. He is meticulous. We have been harmless as doves, but we have omitted the "wise as serpents" part. Revealing the Kingdom to the world will require us to be both.

I believe being wise as serpents looks like bringing forth excellence in solving people's issues and problems—giving them answers that are superior to what they are able to get themselves. It doesn't matter if you are in business or politics, you are providing solutions. When we have answers that solve people's problems, we will start gaining influence and favor and building relationship with the very people around us.

Through this process, we gain trust and we will then have the opportunity to release the dove. People don't care about our Jesus until we are able to bring answers they have been searching for, whether in their personal lives or businesses. When we understand our identity in Christ and allow the Holy Spirit to release wisdom through us to solve the world's problems, we will have an even greater platform to release the dove and demonstrate the love of the Father to the world.

The same thing has happened to our identity. It's been downplayed and minimized to make us smaller than He made us. For us to become what the Father has already made us, we must once again believe in the DNA He put in us and realize we are powerful and able to carry His glory. We've minimized who we are and maximized who we are not through incomplete truths and a misunderstanding of the New Testament and what Jesus did for us. He paid too big of a price for us; playing small just reveals we are still operating out of an orphan spirit in some areas. He wants us to believe we can carry His glory in the world as sons and daughters—equal and one with the Father through what Jesus did for us when he made us one with the Father.

If we thought of ourselves like this, would we believe differently? We wouldn't have problems changing the world and thinking of ourselves as champions. Jesus said the sons of darkness were wiser in their ages than the sons of light (see Luke 16). This scripture bothers, frustrates, and angers me. It's a statement that I believe is a rebuke to the believers and correction to us. I believe this is a statement that represented Jesus' observation of how He saw the sons of light then and how He may still see us today. However, I don't believe we are meant to stay that way. I believe that can be changed, because if it couldn't be, He wouldn't have said that Abraham's sons would be the head and not the tail. I don't know about you, but it offends me to think that the people in darkness are smarter than us when we have the King who created everything living on the inside. To me, it is unacceptable to allow this to remain that way.

How can the world be smarter than the wisdom of the Father? Apparently, we aren't accessing and releasing His wisdom the way He wants us to. We must believe in whom He made us to be so we will access and release His wisdom. Until we begin to approach Him as sons and daughters and believe we are one with Him and allow His wisdom to flow through us to bring answers to the world again, we will continue to be behind the world's achievements.

Why Are We So Behind?

The thought came to me as I began to write one morning, "Why are we so behind?" Why is the world leading in all the systems that God created for His creation to be blessed and empowered? The biggest roadblock is what we think about ourselves, not necessarily what we think about Him. God is looking for people to be on an equal playing field as sons and daughters, to do the things He has commanded us to do in the Great Commission.

We have many examples of how God interacted with the saints of the Old Testament like sons and allowed them to have influence with Him and to speak into His decisions. In Genesis 18:16-33, we see Abraham was approached by God Himself. God says that the evil of Sodom and Gomorrah has come up before Him. But then God says that we (Father, Jesus, and Holy Spirit) should talk to Abraham about what is going on because of the covenant that was made with him. Abraham was going to be great and a Father of nations.

My question is: why would God have to talk to Abraham? Not only did God talk to Abraham, but Abraham bartered with God to find enough people in the city that were righteous so that He wouldn't judge it. If you read the scripture, you will notice that God agreed not to harm Sodom and Gomorrah based upon Abraham's definition of how many righteous might be found in the cities, not based upon His own definition. God said yes to every one of Abraham's requests and was willing to spare the cities. How many of us think we can talk with God like that? Think about Moses. In Exodus 32, we see that God was ready to destroy the people of Israel and start all over with only Moses when the people created the golden calf to worship as their god. Moses stood up to God and told Him that He was wrong and should not kill the Israelites. He provided reasons why God should not do it, and the Word said that God repented or changed His mind. How can a man in the old covenant have that kind of relationship and rapport with the Father? Why don't we think of ourselves like that?

David provides another example in 1 Chronicles 15:17-16:38. David decided he would worship 24 hours, 7 days a week. He was going to send priests in to worship around the Ark of the Covenant. But, this broke the Law of Moses, which stated that the high priest was sent in with a blood sacrifice for the sins of the people only once a year. You can't find where David asked God if it was ok, only that he decided to do it. According to the law, he should have been stoned despite being a king. God never mentions anything about it. How did he do that? I would propose that it was out of the relationship David had with God. I don't think this example supports us breaking the rules because we think it is a good idea. But the question remains, how did these men in the old covenant have such great standing with God, yet we don't see ourselves that powerful with that kind of identity? No one in any of the three stories I mentioned had the new creation living inside of them.

We have allowed ourselves to believe a weak and incomplete truth about our identity from not studying the Word ourselves or being taught by teachers who did not have the full revelation themselves or who may have been fearful to teach the full meaning of being one with the Father. If we understood the completeness of our identity, then we would be more like these Old Testament saints. These men knew that they had a relationship with God Himself. That's what this means. It can't be said any other way. We have a position but have forgotten that we have it, so, we don't act like we do, and we think of ourselves less than who we really are.

These examples are from the Old Testament. In my opinion, we are not even operating at the level of Old Testament saints. In Hebrew 8:6, the Word of God says that the New Testament is founded on better promises and a better covenant—this means that we should be exceeding the saints in the Old Testament. What Jesus did for us and the inheritance He has provided for us in this life and the one to come gives us access to more than they had access to in the old covenant. I realize that saying we are one with God and made in His class and very image may cause you to roll your eyes and say, "You better watch that teaching and thought. You're going to get deceived or tell people they are like the God who made them." If that's what you think about what being one with the Father means, then you've missed the whole point.

Can you name people you know today who think and act like David, Moses, Abraham, Job, Joseph, Esther, Deborah, Jehu, Caleb, and David's 300 men? The point is that we have lost our identity of who we are in Him, and if the Old Testament saints had this kind of standing and place with the Father, why don't we? He's not looking for robots, slaves, or 'yes' men and women. He's looking for sons and daughters who will rule and reign with Him and rescue and restore the earth and our world. He rescued us out of darkness. He expects us to go and rescue the world systems and disciple nations. He left us in charge whether we're comfortable with that statement or not.

We're behind the world in business because when we do poorly in business or have a bad year or season, we make statements like, "It must be a pruning season. I wasn't humble enough. I haven't prayed enough. I must have missed God. I should've waited longer to hear from Him. The warfare has been too intense and held me back from the promises." These are some things I've heard or I have said in times past before I understood my identity. I asked God, "What does the world do when they fail?" He said, "They don't use Me as their scapegoat when they fail!" That hurt.

While we are making excuses and using God as our scapegoat, a secular business person says, "I didn't outwork my competition or market well enough" or "I should've gotten more sales" or "Our strategy could've been better." Instead of blaming God or the devil, they take responsibility and change the plans and actions they take. He showed me through this that we, in a lot of cases, have been irresponsible with our own gifts and talents. We play the victim and take another trip around the same mountain of playing small. We say, "I need to pray, fast, wait on the Lord, confess more, or get another prophetic word. I need to be humbler, I need to sow more money or I need to make new commitments to volunteer, THEN I will get God's favor to prosper in my life and business." That is total B.S. (Belief Systems).

You need to get out there and work to out-produce the competition through strategic plans, actions, marketing, and hard work. You cannot wait or rest your way to a prosperous business. I know that in some cases we've been taught this. That's not what the sons of darkness teach, and Jesus said they were smarter than us. We must adjust, and it should make us mad that He made that statement. We have to start believing in who we are in Him and get our identity back from the incomplete truths we've been brought up in and the religious thoughts that don't have the Holy Spirit's breath and life.

We must realize that we are one with the Father—joint heirs. We have been seated with Christ Jesus in heavenly places on His throne. We are royalty. We are princes and princesses, and we have been made kings, priests, and ambassadors for Him in this life. We are part of the Ecclesia—the governing culture from heaven. We are restorers of the breach. We are repairers, building cities and nations. We have been given the right and authority to reign with Him in this life and the one to come. We are the bride that will sit on the throne beside Jesus Himself. We have to believe this and act like it so we can save the world systems that the Father loves.

For some reason, we think we will only rule with Him in Heaven. We push most of the promises and things that we could do in this life into heaven. Again, if you think that the Father is going to put an untested bride on the throne beside Jesus after the price He paid, and what He suffered for to buy you back, you are wrong. Period. The Father is a great steward of everything He created. He says that He won't even pour the new wine into an old wineskin because it will bust and it will be lost. He's not going to allow us to rule with His Son with something so important as the world until we are ready.

It's time for us to get practice in ruling and reigning here and saving the world because we can. He has given us His authority to fix things. We must start seeing ourselves as the answer to the world's problems and as ruling heirs of the king. We say Jesus is the answer to the world's problems. Well, unfortunately, He's not here. You are, in His stead. He wants to give the answers He has to the world through you. If you don't show up, He won't show up. I want to say it again. If you think the Father is going to put you in charge of something in heaven and you can't even do it here on earth, you are wrong. Why would He? If you aren't faithful with little, why will He give you much? To whom much is given, much is required.

The Kingdom is built a little at a time. Isaiah 28:13 says, "Precept upon precept, percept upon percept, line upon line, line upon line, here a little and there a little." Jesus and the Father won't even waste the wine (Matthew 9:17). Why would they waste stewardship? He's not going to give untested people more responsibility. If we want more of anything in our life, we have to go get it. Stop waiting. Our potential and the things we ache for in this life are in large part unpacked by how well we do our relationship with the Holy Spirit and follow Him. When He tells us to do something, we ought to do it. It is time to restore your identity so you will go and change the world.

We have become weak and ineffective, and we aren't playing at the level at which the Father has called us to play. You may be thinking, "I'm not weak and ineffective." You may not be, but I believe as the whole body of Christ, we are. Let me ask you a few questions and you can decide if what I'm saying has merit. In how many of the spheres in society (Education, Arts, Hollywood, Wall Street, Government,

Media, Economics, Family, Religion) do the thoughts and values of our faith exist, and are the primary thoughts and spirit behind them? How many of these spheres in our country beat with the Father's heart and have His spirit working through them? How many nations have we discipled and are producing Godly values over that nation? If you answered none, you're right. If it were so, they would look different, and we wouldn't be losing the cultural war and wars in our nations. Why are we accepting things as normal in our country that God says are sin?

I could go down the list, but you don't need me to. Just watch the news for a month and then tell me who's in charge. You probably only need 24 hours. It's not the Father or us, but the wrong spirit controlling people. To win, we have to change this. Psalms 115:16 says the earth has been given to men, and in Romans 8, we see that when the sons of God manifest correctly, the very nation and land is healed. This isn't for the next life, but life here and now. What if you and I are the answer to the world's problems? What if we are supposed to take possession and ownership of the world and govern as He would with the heart of serving humanity with the best of the Father? What would it look like if we accepted the charge He left us? I believe there are already people put in place by the Father who are ready and prepared for this cause now.

Joel 2:1-12 describes a people that will perceive the timing of the Holy Spirit when He starts restoring through this unique group. Also, Paul's writings in Romans 8:19-21 gives us some insight in what will happen when the sons of God show up and manifest life correctly so they can bring transformation and healing to entire cities and nations. According to the Word, this has the potential to heal the land and creation itself as a movement of sons and daughters who know how to bring the Father's answers to a dying world. I know that when we start teaching this and thinking this way, there's always a chance of people pushing too far, just like the prosperity message in the 1970's and 1980's where the Father was trying to break the spirit of poverty off His people. Many people went after it, and some produced errors because the message started measuring maturity based on money in a bank account, the size of a home, cars, or jewelry. Obviously, that's not true and it causes people to have error. One of my mentors says that because this happens, the church almost always creates another error to avoid the original error. We start teaching that it's not okay to have wealth or material things. Whenever God does something new, there will always be messes to clean up. But don't stop believing what the Word says because people don't understand it or create a doctrine of error where they push too far a truth He is starting to highlight.

As long as we think He is wonderful and that somehow we are less than He says we are, we won't attempt to do great things with Him. The Bible is full of examples of who He says you are. I won't go through the full list, but you are called a King and a priest, and you've been seated with Him. You're called to be the bride of Christ, to sit beside Jesus Himself. You're called a joint heir with Christ. You've been given the keys of the Kingdom. You can speak on His behalf.

Before I bring this chapter to a close, I want to discuss two primary issues that will cause us to fall from our place with the Father which are highlighted in Ezekiel 28:2-5 and Mark 10:23-30. These two scriptures deal with the issues that are a caution light to us in the scripture to ensure that we won't go there as sons. The first one is our heart being lifted up. You'll see in Ezekiel that King Tyree was being judged by the Lord because his heart had been lifted up which meant that it was lifted up beyond the measure of his creation and capacity. The reason Lucifer fell was because his heart was lifted up beyond the capacity of his creation—not that his heart was lifted up. There's a difference. He was created as an angel. He had a task, and that was his capacity from the Creator. If your heart gets lifted beyond the measure of your creation and capacity, you aren't going to be in a good place with the Lord.

This is what happened to King Tyree. Your heart doesn't need to be lifted up beyond the creation of your own capacity. It is only because of Jesus inside of us that our capacity is unlimited, and it cannot be pushed beyond boundaries as long as we stay in our anointing, gifting, and the multi-layers of that calling. In the first chapter of Joshua, you will see that the promised land is mentioned and it says that you need to go here, there, etc. It gives borders. They were given the land wherever the sole of their feet stepped within those borders. If you get outside of the parameters of the will of God, your capacity, and you get outside those boundaries of what He has put you in, you are operating without Him. You can't put your foot wherever you want and say it belongs to you. It has to be in context of the parameters God has put in your life. Part of your heart being lifted up is making sure your relationship with the Father is current and fresh. Make sure you have people in your life that can be a sounding board and can speak into your life to keep you from being in a place where your heart is lifted up.

In the second scripture, Jesus deals with the trust issue. In Mark 10:23-27, Jesus was teaching about riches. The disciples were bothered by His answer which was, "It is easier for a camel to go through the eye of a needle than for a rich man to enter into the Kingdom of God." The disciples were perplexed, confounded, and confused. When He said, "With God, all things are possible, and with men things are impossible," then they looked at themselves in confusion. They asked, "Then who can be saved?" The answer to what they were thinking was in the question. They had been taught all their lives that the blessings of Abraham should be theirs and part of that is wealth. Now Jesus appeared to be saying that's not how it is and that it may be bad for you. Their thoughts, in my words, are this: "Based on your theology, Jesus, no Jews are going to be saved." What Jesus says next is the critical point. He replied, "Those that trust in riches will not inherit the Kingdom of God."

So, we find out that the unlimited resources of heaven can flow through you as long as your trust stays in the Father. It should always be checked. It's a fine line. The amount that you can handle will stop when you start trusting in it. The two primary issues that caused Lucifer to fall (and can also cause us to fall) are our hearts being lifted up beyond the capacity of their creation and putting trust in things (the created) instead of God, the Creator.

Humility

I know I said I would like to deal with two primary issues before closing this chapter, but there is one more issue to discuss. God has been dealing with me about this one: make sure you keep your heart and being in check with humility. Humility is restrained strength. Philippians 2:8-9 says Jesus did not think it was robbery to be equal with the Father, but He humbled Himself to the death of the cross. Humility is defined in Paul's writings about Jesus.

Jesus had superior strength, but He humbled Himself to the will of the Father. Jesus had a choice to go to the cross because He was perfect and never sinned. He could have lived as a human with God living inside of Him, and never died because He never sinned. Then the Christ would have been in only one body for eternity. We see Jesus humble Himself to the will of the Father in the garden of Gethsemane when Jesus prayed, "O My Father, if it is possible, let this cup pass from Me; nevertheless, not as I will, but as You will." Jesus could have made the choice to not go to the cross, but "He humbled himself to the death of the cross." Humility was a restraint of Jesus's will and strength.

Humility isn't being weak or thinking less of ourselves as many of us have been taught. Humility is when we have a strength or superiority in one area and we restrain it and submit to His will. If we let humility be our guide and restrain our strength when He says to, not allow ourselves to be lifted up beyond the capacity of our creation, and keep our hearts trusting Him when the resources come, we won't fall. We can accomplish these things when we allow people to speak into our life, study His Word, and have a life of communion with the Father.

The Father can release unlimited resources if we keep our hearts within His boundary for us and we continue to trust Him regardless of His blessing. You set the limit of resources you're able to have, handle, and manage based on your identity, heart, and how well you are growing in Him and the maturity to handle the resources. The Father wants to release unprecedented influence and wealth to you to win and disciple nations as sons and daughters. People with transformed identities, who know who they are, can do great things with Him.

Until we stop creating our Christian experience as some sort of "bless me" club that says, "I'm good, you're good, great to see you, see you next Sunday," and break the culture that we only want our people safe, protected, and blessed, we won't change anything. We were built for risk and apostolic adventure—to push the limits, change the systems, and transform the world. But this causes a lot of discomfort and will push us out of our comfort zones. The risk is we avoid the pain. As Edmund Burke said, "All it takes for evil to prevail is for good men to do nothing."

How much more of our country do we have to lose before we stand up and do something? We have to see ourselves as the champions that God has created us to be. Our identity will reveal itself by what we think about Him. In Matthew

16:14-19, Jesus asked the disciples, "Who do men say that I am?" And then He drilled that down to "Who do you say that I am?" Because who they said He was revealed their identity, not His. What you think about Him becomes your identity, and through the right identity, the gates of hell will not prevail and the world systems will not win because you are there to prevent it. The knights will prevent the evil from overtaking our land.

The knights are rising. Our cities are diminishing and collapsing because our light has been hidden and our salt has lost its savor. We must return to the gates of conflict and to the battle for the souls of our cities. Join me in reclaiming our identities as heirs and joint heirs with Him. Our cities, states, and nations are waiting for us, His sons and daughters, to manifest His heart and His answers. I believe He is raising up a group of people that will accept His mission. I'm determined to be one of them. I hope you'll join me.

Chapter 5:

SEAL OF PERFECTION– UNVEILING YOUR GIFTS, TALENTS AND ABILITIES

I n Matthew 10:16, Jesus says, "I'm sending you out as sheep among wolves. Be wise as serpents but harmless as doves." I grew up on a farm, and sheep are basically lunch for the wolves because without any help, sheep have no defense against wolves. I've always heard that it's the Shepherd who protects the sheep, and I believe He is well able to do so. I want to state clearly that I believe the Shepherd can step in and protect you, but in this passage of scripture, He is giving His disciples insight that will aid them in living in a system that's not always friendly. Jesus is giving them wisdom to operate and be effective in the world that surrounds them.

He started unpacking some things to me out of this and other scriptures, and this is where the foundation of my understanding of this revelation started. He is unpacking revelations to us and showing us how to operate in the world system and be successful at whatever we do in the Kingdom. Success is dependent upon the wisdom the Father gave us. Jesus said, "be wise as a serpent," so that means there is something that the Father gave the serpent that we need in order to operate successfully in the earth as sheep among wolves. I began to see that it was the wisdom itself that He gave to the serpent, because that's what Jesus said.

Don't jump ship; stay with me. I felt the same way. The problem is that He wouldn't stop talking about it to me, and He started bringing fresh thought I hadn't previously considered. What we need to know is that the wisdom the serpent had actually came from the Father. It wasn't his own, it was given to him. You can read what wisdom looks like from the Father's perspective in Proverbs Chapters 8 and 9. Before Lucifer himself corrupted the wisdom, it was perfect. In Matthew 10:16, He gives us our divine directive on how to operate in the world system as He intended.

I began to see that when we can't and don't understand a certain scripture, we tend to either dismiss it or make it fit into what we have been taught by other well-meaning people. When we do either, we diminish the power of the Word of God and lose the very revelation Jesus is bringing. This is problematic because we lose the power to be effective in the world. We develop meaning around what He said—meaning that He did not say or intend—from our inability to comprehend it, or inaccurate explanations from well-meaning people. This is dangerous at a minimum and deceptive at the worst, even if our lack of understanding is unintended. We should embrace what the Word says, and when it causes mystery and we don't understand, we have to trust that either the Lord will give the understanding, or we have to be okay with the mystery. We must not try to explain something that we don't yet have insight into.

The Lord packed into His systems how we would be successful in operating in the world. We have to change our operating system in our nations if we want to be effective again. Because we have not known how to engage the world, we have surrendered all the systems of thought and spheres of influence to darkness in our nations. The Ecclesia has backed away from society by and large and we are not effective. Although evil existed at the turn of the 20th century in America, most of the values at the top of the systems were still founded on a God-based value system. Over 100 years later, it has become a mess. People don't even know what gender they are. What has happened? How do we fix it, and how do we restore it back to the way the Father intended? If you disagree with my assessment that we have lost the spheres of influence, point to just one in which our values are the predominant thought and culture.

The Seal of Perfection

Let's begin to unpack a large part of how to get back into what the Father's intent was from the beginning. Ezekiel 28 says, "You were the seal of perfection." The Lord started showing me this part of what is in us and the substance the Father put in us that David talked about in Psalm 139:13-18. He started showing me that this substance had the seal of perfection in it.

Part of this seal of perfection is made up of our gifts, talents, and abilities. Your seal of perfection gives you a certain bend toward precisely what God created you for. If we operate these gifts, talents, and abilities, and bend by being wise as serpents in the world, we will be shrewd and start doing business in the world as God intended. In Luke 16:8, He said that the sons of darkness are wiser in their generation than the sons of light. I would translate that in our time as "They are smarter than us." When I read those words as the Lord began to open up this mystery to me, I got mad. I said, "This shouldn't be." Then, I finally began to be open to what He was revealing. I realized that Lucifer was perfect, and he was in the garden. We were perfect and from the garden. He started showing me that some of our destiny is similarly packed in us. The insight that Jesus gives in Matthew 10-16 shows our identity as sheep, but that we are to be wise as serpents in the world, and to ultimately release the influence of the dove, or the Holy Spirit.

We are sons and daughters. We are created in the same class and species as He is; we are created in His image and likeness. The Lord started showing me that we are packed similarly in a sense that the seal of perfection, wisdom, and beauty is packed in the substance that David referred to in Psalm 139:13-17, "For you formed my inward parts, you covered me in my mother's womb. I'm Fearfully and Wonderfully made. Marvelous are Your words, and that my soul knows well. My frame was not hidden from you when I was made in secret and skillfully wrought in the lowest parts of the earth. Your eyes saw my substance being yet unformed. And in your book, they all were written. The days fashioned for me when as yet there were none of them."

The seal of perfection encompasses our gifts, talents, and abilities that were put in us before we were formed. Psalm 139 says, "He was forming us in our mother's womb. As we were yet unformed, there was a substance placed in us." He showed me that the word substance has a connection with Hebrews 11 where it says that faith is the substance of things hoped for—that actual substance is His DNA. And within His DNA, there are many things. I'm only focusing on these three things for now: the seal of perfection, wisdom needed to exert what that seal will produce, and then the beauty that comes forth out of that.

We are unpacking the first one right now. We were skillfully worked and wrought. That seal is in us—the substance that He put inside of us. Where He put the seal of perfection, which represents our gifts, is related to our "big yes" that resides inside of us and with our divine manifest obsession. You were born with something to do that burns in you—something that serves your natural bend from the Father. Many times, the Father will start showing us things that we are gifted to do and that is in our hearts, and part of our dream mixes through our prophetic potential. However, most of the time, it takes us growing into the people we need to be before we can do what we were born to do. I like what Bill Johnson says, "The reason the Father prunes us is to keep the blessing that He pours out on us from killing us." To have the Father give answers to the very thing we were born for, the thing we were created for, we have to grow up into sons and daughters who can handle it.

Wisdom

Your very occupation and attempt to restore and reform the world and systems are in direct relation to how you unpack The DNA He placed in you and the full sum of wisdom which is put beside your seal. Why? Because we're going into systems that have men in them, and in many cases, have thoughts that oppose the Kingdom. Our job is to convert these systems back to Kingdom values. These gifts, talents, and abilities were put in you pre-packaged and pre-scripted to answer the world's questions.

The instruction He gave us was to be wise as serpents, which is the Father's wisdom, so that we can win cities, people, systems, and the world. Jesus tells His followers that once you are born again, you are to influence like He does. Then, He says, "I am sending you as sheep among wolves." The only way to survive in that environment is to be wise as a serpent. The world and the people out there are like serpents, so when they see you operating and being wise as the serpent, they will think you're like them. What they don't know is that you're carrying the Dove. You are one with Him, not a serpent.

I know you are thinking, "That can't be right," but Jesus said it and you can't get around Him. He is the Word made flesh. I have no problem with this after several months of receiving insight from the Father. As I began to write, the revelation grew larger and clearer to me. In Matthew 10:16-

18, He is saying that as you are in the world, you are among wolves; in verse 18, He says, "Beware of men." I think His instruction is that in the world you must be wise as a serpent, or you will likely die before your time. He explained it to me like this: your identity is in Him and you will use the influence as the dove when it's time, but in the world, be wise as a serpent.

Here are some examples of what that might look like in the world. Before going to see Pharaoh, Joseph shaved his beard (Genesis 41:14). In Leviticus 21:5 and 19:27, it says for Jewish men not to do this because it breaks the law of Moses. Was Joseph compromising or being wise as a serpent? In Esther Chapter 4, it says that Esther had to go before the king, and if you were not summoned, the penalty could be death, She had to reveal she was a Jew to try and save her people. I would recommend that you read the whole chapter, but the statement you have probably heard is, "Who knows whether you have come to the kingdom for such a time as this" (Esther 4:14). Let's look at David who came to national prominence by killing Goliath. Did you know that no one knew who he was and that his father didn't even invite him to the feast where Samuel was coming to anoint the next king? The word is replete with this theme. Moses was hidden as a baby, no one knew who Daniel was until it was time. How about Gideon, Jehu, Deborah, Elisha? How about Jesus Himself? No one knew who He was until He was 30 years old. He was hidden.

The kingdom of God is built around His timing. Ecclesiastes 3:13 states, "He has made everything beautiful in its time." In James 3:13-18 and Proverbs Chapters 8-9, the Word tells us how to measure where the wisdom is coming from, and if it's His or the world's. Being wise as a serpent involves us being shrewd and sharp in the world, using sagaciousness in our movement and plans (which means having or showing acute mental and spiritual discernment), and being keen and practical in our dealings with the world. We have overlooked one of the greatest truths He has revealed. I've never heard anyone teach in depth on this subject and I understand why! We don't want to be like the serpent. We are like the Father. Remember it was His wisdom, not Lucifer's.

World Systems

About a year before I started writing this book, God started teaching me about the Ecclesia and how they need to be worldlier. I've already expressed my initial reaction to this, but additionally, I said to the Lord "Why do you give me these topics?" He said, "Because that's what needs to happen." I began to tell Him that they are not going to be able to receive this because of the current political correctness and hyper-grace charismatic-isms in which we live. He said nothing more and continued to unpack more revelation to me than I'd ever seen or heard before. I had two choices: dismiss what I was being given or write the book. Obviously, you see the choice I made.

When we begin to understand what He meant when He made this statement and His thoughts on this subject, we begin to have influence in the systems. Through the seal of perfection that's in us individually and corporately, we would begin to shift the world systems. When our seals of perfection are expressed correctly, it solves problems in the world. The substance from the Father—His DNA—is packed within our seal of perfection.

When we unpack it correctly, we will have the answers to the questions the world is asking. We will fix problems through influence, not imposition. We will gain favor with those in the world system. The world doesn't care about your Jesus! They also don't care if you're a Muslim, man, woman, child, adult, etc. What they care about is answers to their problems, and if you can provide answers, you will gain influence and favor no matter your gender, nationality, or religious belief. The world is after answers to *their* problems, not yours or the ones you think they need.

When we can bring answers in this way, we will enable things to work and solve problems for them without our agenda being shoved down their throats. When this happens, you will gain influence and favor through the answers that the Father gives you. They will believe in you because your answers to their questions provide the right solution. But this isn't how we've been doing it. We either come in as doves, quoting scripture and completely turning the people in the world systems off, or we come in with false humility or weakness that does not appeal to the world at all. If we force our agenda or try to hide it through religion, without even caring enough to at least attempt to solve their problems with His superior answers, we immediately lose any influence or credibility.

We have been rude in many ways in our Christian beliefs. We push and pedal our beliefs to the world like a commodity. The Father loves the world so much that He will give them answers to their problems before they even accept Him. He is seeking those of us interested in saving the world, nations, and people. God is calling us to become more cunning and shrewd with the ability to be wise. The difference between us and the serpent is that when we get favor and influence, we know it is Him, and when the timing is right, we reveal the dove.

It's interesting that when Joseph went to see Pharaoh from prison, it says that he cleaned himself up and shaved. Leviticus 19:27 and 21:5 says that Jews were not supposed to shave their beards because it was a part of their identity as Jews. When Joseph went up to give the dream to Pharaoh, he looked like them. Was it wisdom or compromise for which he shaved his beard? I think it's evident that it was wisdom because suddenly he found himself in charge of a nation, their finances, and he answered only to the pharaoh. In one day, he went from the prison to the palace and became second-in-command of the largest nation of commerce that the world knew at the time. He also had the answers that the world needed—he carried the solution that saved the nation of Egypt as a whole and that saved Israel from famine. The Egyptians loved him so much that when he died, the pharaoh and all of Egypt mourned longer for him than his own people.

The cunningness and shrewdness that comes by us properly exercising our wisdom will cause us to move into the world systems with answers. As we gain favor and influence, we will be effective in the spheres of influence. People will trust us because we have superior wisdom and we bring to them not only the answers to their questions that they're asking, but even more. We were built to have answers for the world from the Father. As we grow into becoming the sons and daughters of the King, He will begin to give us insight to restore the world He loved. Our maturity in this process is paramount so we don't forget where these answers are coming from, and so we don't begin to think that it's all about us and lose sight of our connection with the Father. Jesus went through the same process. In Luke 2:52, it says that He increased in stature and favor with God and man.

Jesus was just as much the Son of God when He was a baby as He was when He was 30 years old in His identity. However, His maturity as a Son was developed over thirty years before The Father said, "This is my beloved Son in whom I'm well pleased." You, like Jesus, have to grow up. Jesus grew in favor and wisdom until the time appointed by the Father. Why did He have to be tested in the wilderness by Satan? It was part of His process to be able to stand under what the Father wanted to pour out upon Him and through Him. We have to grow up and mature to handle the blessing of the Lord as well. Without our own wilderness experiences, we wouldn't be able to carry the answers He wants to give the world.

Jesus was the first born among many brethren. This means that He was to be the example of what it was like to be a man full of the Spirit of the Father. In Galatians 4:1, Paul gives us insight into this by saying, "As long as the heir is a child, though he be Lord of all, differs nothing from a slave but is under mentors appointed by the Father until the time comes." Jesus was never a slave—we were, and He covered every part of our life here as sons through His identification with us. We were slaves to sin based on Adam's transgression, and Jesus paid for everything and identified with us, so we could be free. He was crucified, buried, and raised. Why? So that we could live out His life here on earth as the Father intended. He learned obedience as a Son through the things He suffered. Our destiny requires us to grow up in Him so that we can manifest His perfect design through our dreams and desires from the Father being expressed. When you are born again, you are just as much a son or daughter of God as you will ever be—a new creature. Like it says in 2 Corinthians 5:17, "Old things have passed away and all is new." In order to mature we need to grow in our relationship with the Father. Romans 12:2 says that we are transformed by the renewing of our mind. As this happens, you grow up just like Jesus did into a mature son or daughter of God, able to champion what He put into your heart.

The path is the same as His. You have to be tested and tried to see if you can stand under the weight of the desires that the Father placed inside of you. Jesus desired nations—that's a lot of weight. If you read Ezekiel 28, you read that Lucifer was created with a certain capacity, purpose, and design by God, and when he decided to step outside of his original creation as an angel, he couldn't stand up under the weight of that decision and he fell. The point here is within the substance where your gifts and talents exist, you must cooperate with the Holy Spirit, the Teacher, to be developed and matured.

There is a time appointed by the Father for you, in each season you go through, to mature you in your walk with Him. When we join Him in unpacking the potential He placed in us, we empower those around us. Some of the answers that the world needs are in the people you lift up and empower. Their answers may be even greater than yours. Some of David's mighty men killed two to three times more giants than David did. As you become a fully empowered son and daughter with His ring and robe of authority, through your growth and appointment from the Father, blessings and answers will come from Him. But with that comes opposition. Your dreams and desires will be tested. You will find in James 1:1-3 that our faith is always tested. Mark 11:23-24 says that whatsoever you desire when you pray, believe them and you will receive them.

So, we see that faith is actually birthed out of desire; through desire realized, we experience a part of the tree of life (Proverbs 13:12). When life shows up, death leaves. When we step into our destiny, it can remove darkness from the people around us. In Matthew 8:29, Jesus simply shows up and darkness has to leave. In Acts 17:4-6, wherever the apostles went, the cites were turned upside down. This is proof that as we grow up into fully empowered sons and daughters and release what He put in us, the DNA from the Father can dethrone darkness through us.

Most of the people I talk to who are believers expect to bypass the process of growing up and maturing in the gifts they've been given. They have misconceptions around the prophetic words that they've been given and think that somehow the Father is going to magically snap His fingers and it will appear without any action on our part. They have a misunderstanding of what resting and waiting should look like. Our rest begins in faith and trust. Faith without works is dead. Rest isn't based on inactivity but is lived out while in the middle of moving towards our destiny. Most of my walk with the Father, in business and in growing up in life, has shown me that He is always waiting on me to grow up into the son who can handle what He is wanting to pour out on me and through me.

Thoughts and Actions

The biggest reason the world has more wealth than us (which I measure by the word currency—meaning money, favor, influence, power) is because they outwork us. If you do a comprehensive study of Proverbs, the book of wisdom, you will find that work, prudence, discretion, perseverance, wisdom, understanding, correction, and discipline are major themes of a successful life.

You will begin to develop long-term, forward thinking as you find and work out the seal of perfection in you. I told one of my closest friends, Dan Colvin, that the world tends to look at longer timelines to measure improvement. People tend to use three- to five-year views, and most look out over a decade for longer term goals and accomplishments if they are forward thinkers. Usually the foresight for many of us as believers has been short-term at best—one to two years at most. Our view of inheritance and promise has been limited by short-term vision for what Jesus paid for. His finished work has given us unlimited potential to change the world, yet we still believe that we are simply supposed to occupy this world until He comes back! What if instead of thoughts and plans of leaving, we started making plans for a hundred years out, and begin envisioning what type of world we want to leave for our great-great-great-grandchildren? This mind-set will empower you to explore more in life and to create wealth for generations because there is a purpose beyond your life for it.

The actions you take are more important than the vehicle through which you choose to create wealth in the beginning. I didn't say the vehicle wasn't important at all, but if it matches your seal of perfection, it's probably a good option to consider for creating wealth. If we would go after something for a decade instead of one year, work our butts off, learn from failure, and adjust through the feedback we receive, then take new actions moving forward, we would start to gain the success that we envisioned.

It took ten years in our business for me to be able to take a week's vacation and have my wife able to stay home to raise our first daughter. Before that, we only took vacations on long weekends and my wife had to work a full-time job. A decade of hustling, receiving feedback, learning what didn't work, and taking new and more actions allowed us to achieve financial stability, and I could somewhat predict what was coming next in my business. One of my mentors says, "It takes 25 years to become an overnight success."

It takes time to uncover the seal He placed in you. It's like mining gold out of your heart, it normally doesn't just come automatically.

Your dreams and desires have to be tested because faith is birthed out of them, and faith is always tested. According to James 1:2-5, God allows the test for you to grow up and expand to see if you can handle it when it comes. Bill Johnson says, "All increase is rewarded with pruning." Pruning is required so that when your blessing comes, it doesn't kill you. John C. Maxwell has written some of the best material on leadership in our time. Maxwell states in his research that on a scale from 1-10 (one being the lowest and ten being the highest), people can usually grow two spots. Consider your talents. If you're a three in one task or activity, based on his research, you will only become a five even when you work hard at it. But when you're a seven at something and work hard, you can become a nine. When you start working on the gifts and talents inherent in your seal of perfection, you can become a nine. When you become a nine in your gifts and talents and bring excellence through them, the wisdom then flows over them. As John C. Maxwell says, "People will stand in line for nines." Read more about this in John C. Maxwell's book *The 21 Irrefutable Laws of Leadership: Follow Them and People Will Follow You.*

In other words, you will have influence. We come pre-packaged with a few talents that are unique to us, and we are already a seven in those particular areas. If you discover, uncover, and grow into those talents, you will start realizing who you are and will walk through this process naturally.

Sometimes these processes are hard and can take more time than we thought they would. This is where we must stay the course and persevere.

Did you realize that you have a signature sound and as you mine it through your gifts, you start producing the sound and it flows through you and produces excellence? Your signature sound comes through your seal of perfection. Our sound is made by the two or three talents and abilities we are already really good at. That seal has things in it that, once developed, can naturally make you look like a genius. Just like the Father. People might say, "You do that really well," and you think nothing of it because it comes naturally to you. This is the point. This is part of the seal in you. You only need to become proficient in one or two of your gifts to be successful. When these gifts and talents are developed, they provide answers to other people in their lives. They also become a catalyst to reveal the Kingdom to others. Your signature sound has a wind of the Spirit on it. People will start coming to you for the answers you carry to the world around you. When this happens, the Father will show up in their lives because of you.

Influence and Favor

I found out years ago that as I developed and accessed this substance from the Father, I could immediately provide the answers that people were seeking through the gifts that were in the sound and seal inside me. I immediately had influence and favor. I learned in that season that it's easy to disciple the world, but our challenge as believers is to actually step into who He created us to be and start doing it. The Lord gave me new insight when He revealed that the main reason the world and Jewish people are ahead of us in creating wealth and accomplishing dreams and desires is because we do not have a complete understanding of the New Testament. The inheritance He provided for us by His finished work has given us access to so much more than we are currently experiencing. The New Covenant has superior answers and wealth beyond our current level of understanding. We have been made Royalty, Kings, and Priests! His finished work provided so much for us. Let us explore and go in deeper to find this great wealth that has been given to us.

The Word says that the New Testament is established upon better promises and better covenant than the Old Testament, so that means it's superior. Hebrews 8:6 reveals this insight. The Lord started showing me this, and the truth of it altered the destinies of the people with whom I shared it. I had a friend and mentor in my workout group who was not a believer, and he found out I was a Christian, so he started asking me some questions. One question he asked was, "Do you believe in dinosaurs?" Instead of arguing with him and trying to prove a point, I simply said, "Yeah, I do." He was immediately confused because I wouldn't argue with him— by then, I had learned not to do that. He and I continued to build a relationship over a couple of years, and one day he told me that he had to make a decision that would alter his family's destiny. He was considering different options to create more income to support his family—one option was moving to New York City and being a stock trader. I asked him, "What do you think about it?" He said he wasn't sure and that he liked living in North Carolina and didn't want to move up North.

The next week while we were running, he mentioned it again, and I could feel the anguish and uncertainty in his voice. I felt compassion and empathy for him and his family, and suddenly I heard these words come out of my mouth: "Here's what you do. Next time you ride your bike in the woods, lay down in the leaves, look up to Heaven and ask the Father what to do, and He will tell you." I ran off ahead of him so that he couldn't have time to respond, and I thought to myself, "Where did that come from?" I hadn't planned to say that. We finished our run, and neither of us said a word. It was awkward. I remember saying to the Lord, "If you don't talk to him, I'm going to look like a fool." I couldn't believe that I had said that. I was worried because I knew that he was going trail riding later that day, and I thought, "What if the Father doesn't say anything? What if all the trust I had gained with him disappears because of this?"

That night I received a text message from him and I thought, "Ok the moment of truth is here!" I hesitantly opened the message and read, "I got my answer." I texted back immediately and asked, "What did he say? What happened in the woods? Give me the details." No response at all, but I knew I would see him at the gym the next day.

He never said exactly what happened or what was said. All he told me was, "I got my answer." In that moment, I realized the power of that statement. The entire world is looking for is answers to their questions, and if you can get answers from the Father to them, it will have an eternal impact because the answers are directly from the Father. This is part of your seal of perfection. Develop yourself in such a way that you receive insights from the Father on behalf of others, and are able to give the world answers.

I've had several similar interactions since my encounter with the Lord that I shared at the beginning of this book. I've been a part of people being healed of various ailments. My point is that learning who we are and learning how we flow in the Father through our seal of perfection will allow us to access answers greater than we already have. When we know who we are and know we have substance in us from the Father, His answers flow through us naturally, which creates favor and influence. By giving away the best of Him through me, I've given answers to people around me.

Your Potential

To achieve your potential, it is your responsibility to unpack your prophetic potential and the gifts, talents, and abilities wrapped in the seal. Bill Johnson says, "The Father is not going to complete your potential for you. That's your job." When we do our part to uncover and discover what these gifts and talents are and what is unique to us, we will see them come through us. Then we will see the God part in it.

When you understand this, you realize that everything you will ever need is inside you. All that you need to complete your potential is inside of you right now, but it's up to you to mine it out like gold. Most people never discover their potential, talents, and abilities. Part of your destiny is wrapped up in God—what He put in you and how He leads you. The other part of your destiny is wrapped up in you and your willingness to go after it with everything you have, so that your potential can be completed like He planned.

Before I understood this, I would postpone realizing all my potential for when I get to Heaven. Most of us still shove all the prophetic promises and inheritances in the Word to Heaven at a future date, or we put all the responsibility on God to make it happen. If it doesn't happen, we blame Him. God showed me that we have to take responsibility for our own seal of perfection. Our inability to unpack what He put in us is a big problem. I came to this realization about thirteen years ago and it changed everything. I started doing my part so that He could do His. Faith requires us to move first, and then He will move. Faith without work is dead. I developed my gifts and talents through my actions. I worked out my own faith with Him.

Three things that guarantee you won't manifest your gifts and talents are as follows:

1. You push them out to the future—to Heaven
2. You push all the responsibility of your prophetic potential on God and not yourself
3. You bury the talent in your heart because you're too afraid to do anything with it

If you do any of these three things, you will not fulfill your potential. The Word says that we are co-laborers with

Him (see Corinthians 3:9.) He wants to co-create with you in the process. You and God each have a part.

When I realized that He put everything in me before I was born, and I have to help to mine it out, everything changed. My prayer life changed. I rarely ask for anything unless something is highlighted or I get an unction (which is a sensing or feeling on the inside). While there is nothing wrong with asking, I learned that until the wind of God was blowing in a certain direction for me, it was premature to pursue it with prayer. You will have to work out your own process with the Father in your life's walk.

This doesn't mean I wasn't doing anything. I was busy doing what the Father had shown me prior. As the wind started to blow, I declared what I was sensing, feeling, or seeing, and looked for His direction for what was next. My constant foundation in the process is that I declare what I am seeing and then follow after what the Father is show-ing me to pursue. It normally looks bigger than I think I am and my ability to move into where He is going. So, I began to declare who I am—the man that He has made me to be. About 10 years ago I learned from a mentor, Lance Wallnau, how to develop "I am" statements that keep me clear about my identity.

- I am a son
- I am a world changer
- I am a rescuer of nations
- I am in possession of blueprints and strategies for the world

- I am the Father's son
- I am a wealth creator for myself and others
- I am a giant slayer over my life

These are just a few of my statements. I confess them over myself because they are true and real.

This process helped me unpack my seal, my signature sound—the two or three things at which I am really good. My business exploded to new levels. Not only did I find my strengths, but I found my weaknesses, and I began to delete them from of my life and delegate them to my staff who were better at them than me. In my company, I only do what I'm really good at, and I let my well-equipped staff handle any tasks that I'm not good at, so I can operate in excellence.

It's important to know what your seal is, but it's just as important to know who and what you are not. You can never be who you're not. We can develop the anointing and authority for the things we naturally carry from the Father. Don't be what you are not—be what and who He made you to be.

A certain glory is revealed through your seal. As you develop and begin to go to the top, excel and stand out, this excellence gives you a place at the top of the mountain where your gifts and abilities are seen. Your signature sound is heard, and you gain favor and influence. Promotion starts to flow because there is an irresistible glory that comes on you through the process of becoming who the Father created you to be.

If you live out the seal of perfection long enough to bring forth excellence that is congruent with your gifts and the Father's heart, you will find that it gives you influence to change the world. The glory of the Father will be revealed to the world through the seal that He placed inside of you. Focus on developing your gifts, speaking out your "I am" statements, going after what God has put in your heart, and realizing your prophetic potential. You will start to rise to heights you never thought possible in this life, and you will become a source of answers for the world around you.

Chapter 6:

FULL OF WISDOM

T he substance in you, the DNA from the Father, includes wisdom among many other things. Wisdom is activated by manifesting the seal of perfection—or your gifts, talents, and abilities. Wisdom seems like it's hidden, but when you discover your gifts in you and develop and release them, wisdom starts to flow over them and answers seem to come out of nowhere. Sometimes it feels almost magical when this happens.

Wisdom flows out of the fear of the Lord. Proverbs 9:10 says, "The fear of the Lord is the beginning of wisdom." Wisdom comes through relationship and intimacy with the Father as we begin to walk out with Him the things that He has placed in us. The fear of the Lord is about respect, honor, and being pliable to His heart. 1 Corinthians 1:30 says that Jesus made wisdom unto us. All the wisdom you will ever need is already in you if Jesus is in you.

We will unpack at least three revelations of wisdom that the Father shared with me. When God put His DNA in us, it is perfect just like Him. When Lucifer was created, he was perfect because he was created by the Father, but he fell because iniquity was found in him. The reason I point this out is because we were created in God's image and likeness, in His class as sons and daughters, not angels. But we can use the wisdom and gifting against His original intent the same way we choose not to follow the Holy Spirit. This is a caution light as we move into how He wants us to operate in the earth not to abuse that which He gave us. The fullness of wisdom and the power to execute your gifting is part of the substance God placed in you. In 1 Corinthians 1:24, we see that when we believe, there is a release in us for the power and the wisdom to flow out of us into the world. A shift is coming in how and why we relate to people in the world. It doesn't matter whether it's in your community or in the governor's office. Answers are coming through you.

1 Corinthians 1:19-25 reminds us that the foolishness of the Father is wiser than men. This scripture could say, "…the wisdom of men," instead of "…wiser than men." You will see that this is at the heart of what He is saying. When the wisdom in you is released through the excellence of your talent and abilities being developed in you, you will begin to gain influence and favor through what's coming out of you. This very wisdom is what created the earth and everything you see. It's in you, and it can solve any problem in life. It's our job to unpack and discover it so we can give it out

to those we are called to influence. The Kingdom is built from the inside out, and we must be diligent to mine what is inside of us. The wisdom He wrapped up in you has insight and understanding for you to be successful, but it also has answers for the world around you.

The wisdom from the Father is organic in nature. When wisdom is properly given out, it will shift and change those who receive it. When it comes, it has living and breathing understanding on it. A verse in Proverbs 8-12 says wisdom is defined as "being shrewd, intelligent, and has living under-standing to devise a plan for life." This wisdom encompasses the breath and life of the Father Himself and has the ability to fix any problem, heal anything it touches, and bring free-dom to all who touch it.

As you start believing in what is on the inside of you and start going after the dreams in your heart, wisdom is released to aid you in your journey. The Kingdom is inside you—stewarding what is in your heart is part of what you must do for things to manifest. When you show up with who you are and the identity of a son and daughter in relationship with the Father, then the very nature and wisdom in you has the power to displace darkness when you show up with the answers that it brings. The answers are wrapped up in you, and God's wisdom flowing over it causes the spirits that are not of God to be removed.

Zechariah 1:18-20 shows us that Israel was being con-trolled and the peoples' hearts were being cast down by four horns that are representative of the anti-Christ spirit. Then, four craftsmen showed up. The prophet Zechariah asked,

"What are these craftsmen here for?" The angel says to him, "To displace the four horns." (The King James Version says, "To fray them.") The Word of God says these four craftsmen showed up to fray the enemy. When they showed up, they didn't do anything except what they were called to do, which was build. That anointing on them caused the enemy to be displaced and removed. When you show up, you displace the enemy when the Spirit flows over what you do.

The anointing on the four craftsmen caused the enemy to leave. Your anointing and the wisdom of the Father will do the same thing. 1 Corinthians 1:20-30 tells us that the foolishness of God is wiser than men. How much bigger and better is His wisdom? If we could believe this, we would become the people we were called to be. His wisdom in us is exceedingly beyond what we could ask or think.

I believe that when we show up with our gifts and His DNA inside of us, His power, authority, and wisdom flows out and neuters the enemy and displaces the spirit of darkness. People will be free in your sphere. Acts 17:5-6 gives us a glimpse of this in the early church. It says, "They were powerful and knew who they were, so when they showed up in cities, the cities were disrupted and turned upside down. But the Jews did not believe, moved with envy, took unto them certain lewd fellows of the baser sort, gathered a company, and set the city on an uproar. They assaulted the house of Jason, and sought to bring them out the people, and when they found them not, they drew Jason and certain brethren to the rulers of the city crying these that have turned the world upside down have come here."

We need to start realizing this and acting as if this were true. We must begin to believe in who He created us to be and start showing up with power, or the enemy will continue to rule over people and cause death and destruction in our systems and nations. We will continue to lose the war. We must grow up and go up with His all-encompassing wisdom and ascend to the mountains that we are called to and take ground with wisdom. When you find out the very thing He put in you, develop it, and allow wisdom to flow over it, you will be undefeatable. The enemy won't be able to stay where you are.

For centuries, the Kingdom of God has been advanced through force. But this isn't His highest way of doing things. The knights will rise through influence, favor, wisdom, and leadership. We will have the heart to serve and bring the answers of the Father to our cities, and these answers will be superior to those that currently prevail. This will cause conflict, but not because we are causing it or trying to start anything—it is because when His Spirit shows up with His answers, any other spirit unlike His will be removed. When we stand and influence through serving, people who have the wrong spirit will be released from those spirits and given a chance to know God themselves. Then, they will see clearly and be able to choose for themselves. Our job is to show up with His solutions and remain in a state of serving and influence—He will take care of the rest. The scripture reminds us that He sets one up and puts one down. We need to begin to go up with that Wisdom, and we will see that His Wisdom is irresistible.

It's not about creating conflict. When you begin to lead in any area, the DNA inside of you has God's influence on it. When that happens, it causes negative manifestations out of others. Any DNA that's not His is challenged and disrupted. All the conflict today is calling out for the knights to rise, step in, and fix the systems. The crying and anguish in the world is waiting for the sons and daughters of the King to step in and fix it. 1 Corinthians 1:25 says, "The Foolishness of the Father is wiser than men, and His weakness is stronger than men." His Wisdom will give you a different view. Proverbs Chapter 8 includes so much about wisdom—read it for yourself and see these truths being lived out. It begins with a view from the top of the spheres of influence because this is where the gates are located. If you become excellent in what you do, you will find yourself at the top, at the gates, from where the spheres are ruled and governed. It's time to step into the arena to which you are called, and to not step back and let the world get worse. It's time for the sons and daughters of the King to step in; we are the only ones who have the power to change it.

Wisdom produces an understanding heart that will cause a unique sound to come out of you as you develop. Clarity comes through wisdom. Used properly, your insight will give you greater wisdom. Wisdom in your heart becomes a weapon of protection against fear, pride, and arrogance. Wisdom causes you to have strength in all you do. It allows you to lead well, and justice will flow out of you.

Wisdom causes wealth to flow from you—it causes gain. The blessing of the Lord will make you rich and add no sorrow. This wisdom is already inside of you because you are and a new creature. It's about you becoming and manifesting your true self, substance, and DNA from the Father. Wisdom will show up as you unpack it. As you move in this wisdom, the products you make, answers you provide, or services you provide cause others to be blessed because they will have the Father's DNA on them. It doesn't matter what sphere you're in, the wisdom will flow out and have answers for people around you and have eternal impact on their lives. Wisdom flowing through you, and your gifts and talents bringing answers to the world, allows people to get a glimpse of what the Father is truly like.

This gave me a foundation from which to start. I don't know many saints who have done great feats like Moses, David, Abraham, Samson, Joshua, Jehu, Caleb, Deborah, Esther, and the list goes on. These are just a few. Hebrews 11, the Hall of Faith Chapter, has a lot of these stories and you should read some of them yourself. In my lifetime, I've seen our values as Kingdom people eroding with a culture that looks more like Sodom and Gomorrah than Heaven on earth. To think or believe any differently with the current state of our culture, cities, states, and nation as a whole, you would have to be insane, on drugs, or both.

Don't allow the spirit of the world to shut you down. Become a Knight rising and begin to declare that the Father has already won and that He is waiting for us to enact His answers through wisdom. Let us rise once again and realize we have been charged by Him to change the world. It's time for us to be the answer to the world's problems.

Joshua 1:8 says to observe and do. We need to see what the Father is doing, find the things that are on His Heart, and begin to go after them regardless of what the establishment is doing. In 2004, I had a spiritual meltdown and I hit a wall with my spiritual father who I loved, and still love to this day. I rarely preach without thinking about him when I'm done—what he poured in me and what he gave to me. But, where I was going, we could no longer walk together. I was a son to him and I loved the journey that we went on for almost 20 years. I believe he gave me the greatest gift in life which is to be discipled. I will always respect and love him for laying down his life for me and others by what he taught and gave to me.

During my meltdown, God started to teach me through someone in the world. I had this encounter and meltdown at the same time. It reminded me that the wisdom of God is sometimes hidden in strange packages. I saw the Kingdom and God's principles in some of the most unusual places and people He brought in my life. What I was taught set me on a completely new course. The wisdom He brought to me in the beginning of my transition into being a son to Him came from a peak performance coach for fifteen months. Then, He brought spiritual mentors in my life who could help me unpack what He was doing. The thoughts were backed up by the Word. Anything that wouldn't fit into His word and values, I threw out. Like Bill Johnson says, "You learn to eat the meat and spit the bones out."

During the meltdown, I processed, applied what I learned, and searched the scriptures to find foundation in the

Word. Then, in 2006, the Father Himself seemed like He just moved into my house. Everywhere my wife and I went, He was there. I understand He is omnipresent, but this was different. Many times, we were overwhelmed and couldn't function physically. Through mentors in the Kingdom, I started to understand what He was doing and realized that I was a son of the Father. Not just because of their teaching, but because I was having my own encounters with Him. His presence seemed to capture us and sometimes incapacitate us—at home, at work, and on vacation. It seemed there was no place He wouldn't show up.

We can't be free to become who we are created to be until we have our own encounter with the Father and understand His love for us. Wisdom flows out of this intimacy. I felt like I was experiencing a romance with the Father. I never operated in wisdom like this until I had this connection and encounter with Him. Sometimes wisdom comes in the strangest packages and most unlikely places. I urge you to be open to how He brings the encounter. I realized that the Lord had begun to unpack my first twenty years in business, which is a lot of what you are reading. I was being raised in the house of Pharaoh at the same time as I was being taught the Kingdom of God. I had two fathers: one was my spiritual mentor and the other taught me business in the world system. I found over time that I had gotten a glimpse into both worlds.

I had no idea at the time that He would later ask me to teach His people how to be worldly—but, here we are. The doctrine you and I were taught wasn't wrong, but when the

Father highlights something else, we need to move with Him. The problem exists when we don't move with Him. It's hard to leave the good thing that God is doing now to go to the great thing that He is going to do next.

I learned that He set up the systems to not only create wealth and life for us, but also to bring forth the answers the world needs. I saw that the sons of darkness were out-prospering us by cooperating with what the Father had set in motion. In Luke 16:8, Jesus said, "The sons of darkness are wiser in the generation than the sons of light." I began to see that this statement was meant to provoke us to change this. We are the head, not the tail. This is a promise for us in the Abrahamic covenant. The sons of darkness aren't supposed to lead. We are. The Father began to show me things through the world with His validation, and I started to excel in my gifting. Wisdom began to flow over it and expose to me His systems. He wants to bring abundance to His sons and daughters, but we have to understand how to first get it and then be able to keep it. Every time He wants to bring change in us, it usually starts with a contradiction to our current, limited beliefs.

Colossians 1:9 says, "To be full of knowing His will and be full with wisdom and understanding." As I've lived life, I've realized when I ask Him for something that I'm not ready for or can't actually carry yet, He takes me through a process to grow me to the capacity to carry what I asked for and what He wants to pour out.

All change is painful at the beginning because at a minimum, it challenges our current beliefs. Many times, it becomes like the splinter in Neo's brain in the movie *The Matrix*, the stick in the mud, or something inside of your gut that feels unsettled and grates against you. This is an invitation from the Father for what is next. When your dreams and desires start coming out of you, they invite attacks into your life—and we haven't yet grasped that faith is always rewarded with test, trial, and opposition. Faith is birthed out of desire. Your desires will attract what needs to happen in you to be able to carry it out. These are process events that change you.

We need wisdom to know when, what, and how to move next. Over the years, I've learned not to initiate things that I desire until I feel Him highlighting something inside of me. Or, if I start seeing something that He has promised me and it's not working in my life yet, I remind myself that He expects us to live in and experience everything Jesus paid for. Many times, what's in our heart has to be mined and worked out before we can see it manifest—this means pruning, and it can feel like the opposite of what we want. Why? Because desire and what is inside of you brings opportunities to process us and allow us to grow into the next level of maturity. Being ready to receive the very thing you dreamed of is only part of the journey. Most believers I talk to are not going into the mountains that they are called to because they are either waiting on God to move them, or waiting to grow up enough so that they feel qualified.

It's time to understand our identity and who we are in Him and what He's done for us—the seat and authority He has made available to us. Through His wisdom leading us, we can be developed into strong people that become dangerous to the kingdom of darkness. We will not ascend to the place where the gates are in the spheres and bring the Father's wisdom to the world until we know who we are. Wisdom is supposed to place us at the top of the gates. Study Proverbs 8 and 9, Ezekiel 28, Matthew 10, and Luke 16. Process them, and you will begin to rise through His wisdom.

There are only two options for who rules at the gates: us or the anti-Christ. There are no other options. We must rise and take back the systems for which Jesus paid. Embrace the next process that shows up. Allow it to work on and through you for His way of wisdom. When wisdom flows over your gifts, talents, and abilities, you will look perfect in all you do. There is no limit to what He will accomplish through us. He chose to do it this way through the manifold wisdom He placed inside of you. He hid the wisdom to answer some of the world's questions inside of you. He invited you to join Him in the process of becoming the best version of yourself. As this happens, wisdom will flow and begin to restore and rebuild the world around you.

Chapter 7:

PERFECT IN BEAUTY—FEARFULLY AND WONDERFULLY MADE

We begin the final chapter realizing how beautiful the One who created us is. Our beauty comes from His. He became everything we were so that we could be everything He is now. We are fearfully and wonderfully made. He has put His beauty in us. He is the fairest among 10,000. He is the lily of the valley. The Desire of all nations. His wonder has no end. The beauty of His holiness attracts men. Until we begin to develop our seal and the wisdom that flows over His DNA in us, we won't release His glory into the world around us. As we uncover our seal of perfection and the wisdom begins to run over it, they become like power twins—a hybrid of power if you will. What they produce in you makes you attractive. Favor and influence come as it displays beauty on you to the people around you. People say, "There's something different about you," and then you are able to provide answers that they haven't been able to access. His influence through your beauty brings people in contact with Him.

If the people around you aren't feeling a sense of life through the beauty of who you are becoming, and this beauty doesn't start to provide the possibility of more joy, strength, and stability, and create new ceilings for their floors—a legacy for them—then it's probably not connected to the Father's plans and beauty for them. This quote from Emerson sums up the primary way I measure success in my life: "To know even one life has breathed easier because you have lived. This is to have succeeded." We see Lucifer's heart was lifted up because of his beauty. He was given beauty from the Father, and he started worshipping himself and his beauty as being from himself instead of acknowledging God and where his beauty came from.

When we look at our beauty, we need to remember that the Father made it that way, not us. After my encounters, I began to learn how to live in gratitude and thankfulness. It's interesting that He used a peak performance coach in the world to help me start this journey. What He desires for you is written in His love letter to you, the Word of God. Discovering your beauty in its fullness, who He made you to be, and the destiny He put inside of you is uncovered as you walk out your life with the Father.

I believe happiness is a continual pursuit. Proverbs 16:20 says, "Happy is he who trusts in the Lord." Your happiness is based on trust in Him, and from there we begin to live in gratitude and thankfulness.

Most of my life I have been looking for the secret—the magic formula that would make me super successful. I was looking for what things I should do in order to become Mr. Wonderful. Much of what I followed, read, or studied had four or eight steps to this or that, and if I followed those steps, my life would change forever. Some of the things I learned from the principles had an impact in my life and I received some benefit out of them. But as I grew, I realized that 80% of life has to do with your identity, and finding your talents, gifts, and the sum of His wisdom placed by Him. No amount of principles, steps, or strategies to success will replace the first part of the process of becoming who you were destined to be.

After much life, some success, and studying this subject for three and a half decades, I've concluded that 80% of life is in who you become and the beauty that is uniquely you. The other 20% is tools or steps to the destination or destiny. I discovered that as I perfected certain areas, the tools and strategies would start showing up. Most of what I see in the world and the church is people who don't know who they are or what is inside of them. Your beauty will only show up through the process of intertwining the seal of perfection and wisdom that's been put in you. Without this, the beauty of who you are is never seen. The goal is to have the Creator shine through us so we begin to look like Him. 2 Corinthians 3:18 talks about us beholding Him as in a mirror and being transformed into the same image from glory to glory as by the Spirit of the Lord. Beauty is about letting what's on the inside shine through because it has the Father's imprint on it. We are the most beautiful when we look like Him.

When we begin this journey of going after the things He put in us, to discover the beauty that is there, ask yourself these questions:

- What turns you on?
- What lights you up?
- What is beautiful to you?

This is part of who you were made to be. Obviously, we need to make sure what we are going after doesn't violate the Word of God and His Kingdom values. If Jesus is called the Desire of nations, He is beautiful. His sons and daughters should be beautiful as well. We should never shy away from what He has done for us and our identity as royalty, because we are His sons and daughters. The answers to the nation's problems are hidden inside of you because He's inside of you. You can't discover the answers by conforming to anything but Him and who He has made you, regardless of the world or religious ideals that have their root in the traditions of what has been. We should always have forward movement and discover what He is doing now. We must look forward, not backward.

We must find our big yes's in life. As you find these yes's in your heart, it becomes easier to say no to other things. You are called to many things, and focusing only on one will frustrate you when that thing isn't moving like you want it to. I'm called to be a father, a businessman, a husband, a champion maker with blueprints for nations—these are just a few of mine. It is okay to have one primary thing that burns in you, but as you build your life and purposes, they will encompass other yes's in your heart. Your destiny and dreams shouldn't be tied to only one thing. You are much bigger than one yes.

In my journey, I've noticed other people get frustrated when the one big yes isn't working or moving like they dreamed it would. I have done it many times. Work on the things that seem to be highlighted by Him in the season you're in and start asking what you can do to move closer to the other things that burn in you. Keep moving and developing yourself. Life is not about what you gain, it's about who you become in the process. Achievement through personal transformation is the essence of becoming. This is one of my life statements that has kept me moving forward in difficult times and makes me regain my focus when I lose it.

Potential is often discovered somewhat by accident in the beginning. That's what happened to me at the start of my journey. When my potential started being developed on purpose through my talents and abilities being exercised through growth and excellence, it caused me to have greater insight for my clients and give me greater influence with them. It caused the beauty on my solutions to stand out to them. They also developed a trust in me that created a likability factor to do more business with me. As one of my mentors says, "You become sticky and you start attracting the right deals, the right clients, and so on." The three legs that I believe things are built on are:

1. Gifts and talents

2. Desires, dreams and destinies
3. Belief that is attached to purpose

These are your foundations for the Father's DNA to sit on and be released through you to shine. If we aren't careful, the world and people around you will define you and your identity. It's up to us to find out who we are based on the Father's perfect design. When you start developing the first two legs of the foundation, clarity will begin to come in from every direction, and the third leg will be built as you uncover the first two.

Whenever you allow someone else to define your life, it eventually creates misery. It's not the real you. You have to find your path, what makes your heart sing, and what's beautiful to you. As you move by faith toward what's in your heart, you will find what you are attracted to, what lights you up, and what causes your heart to beat faster. When you notice these things, you'll start understanding more of your identity and purpose. This takes time. Keep exploring as you venture out into the world. You may have to do many things in your occupation in the beginning to find your natural rhythm. As you see these gifts and they work in you, you will be naturally drawn to the things you were built for in business and in life. They will always match your DNA from the Father.

This is what creates the beauty of you—when you come alive in the things that inspire you. It takes faith to walk this out. You have to be willing to dig out the gold inside of you. This isn't an easy process because it requires trial and error and working through failure. You must also be willing to receive feedback and start again. When I started my journey, I didn't know what was beautiful to me. It took a while. But as I developed myself, I started realizing what lit me up. It was always connected to my natural DNA. At that time in my life, I attempted to only do those things that lined up with that DNA. This is where I excel the most and where I'm fully alive. Bill Johnson says, "What feeds me, feeds them." As I found what feeds me, I started giving it away, and it started attracting the people that needed what I had or I needed what they had. This is what beauty does.

We have now become the temple of God through the Holy Spirit taking up His residence in us according to the Word (1 Corinthians 6:19). This beauty is to be released through us to the world as sons and daughters of God. Our challenge is to discover what He put in us and the part we play in revealing His beauty in which we become. If He's beautiful, then His offspring should be beautiful. How do you think the world is going to taste and see that He is good? Through His sons and daughters. Everybody wants a King like Jesus. They just don't know it. He is so good, and when revealed correctly, no one can or would resist him. Proverbs 13:12 says that desire realized is the tree of life. Answers to people's questions and desires that resolve their issues create beauty and happiness for them. When you have an answer for them that's tied to their dreams and desires, they can taste of eternity and the tree of life because of the answer that came through you from the Father.

Our agenda should be the Father's (see John 3:16-17). He so loved the world that He gave His Son. Our agenda should be the same—to save and rescue the world and systems from darkness because we have access to answers from Him. "The glory of God is man fully alive." – St. Irenaeus of Lyons. Answers are beautiful and bring life to those who need them. What if the Glory of God on you has answers for people? The answers through us have the power to restore our cities, build up the ruin and broken places (Isaiah 61:4-7).

The Father will give us more answers when we have and understand His heart for the systems that He created and the people He loves. Influence comes when we serve others well with the answers they are asking for, without hidden agendas toward them. When we realize we are able to access solutions for the world around us, the value system of His Kingdom will come with the answers they are wanting. Then, not only will their problems be solved, they also get to taste eternity from the life coming through them because they originate from His heart.

Success Story

John C. Maxwell's teachings are probably one of the highest standards of leadership teaching. Maxwell tells a story when he was meeting with some business people who were getting incredible results in their businesses because of his books and teachings. They wanted to know where and how he found and developed his leadership material. He attempted to dodge the question, but they kept asking. So, he gave them a vague explanation that didn't really answer the question and that they didn't believe. Still trying to move on to another subject, the group wouldn't stop until he answered the question. He finally tried one last attempt by telling them they would not like the answer, but they persisted. So, he finally gave in and said that the foundation of all his material originated from the Word of God.

The point is that they only wanted to know because what he was giving was making their businesses successful. They weren't interested in who he was, but in how and from where he got his leadership material. People are not normally interested in our Jesus in the beginning, but they are interested in you providing them with the answers they seek. If what you have and give them brings them superior results, then you will begin to have influence and they will trust you to open other doors in their life. True beauty comes out of the identity of who you are. What if your actions set a new standard in a sphere? What if walking in your identity has the power in it to disciple the thoughts and values of people in the Kingdom like John C. Maxwell has through his leadership teachings?

It's easy to disciple the world because the world doesn't care who you are. They only are interested in what you bring and the questions and problems you can solve. I began to discover this after I had my life-altering encounter in 2006. It took a few years to start seeing this happen intentionally in my life. I began working out with a new group of guys in 2010, and I noticed at times that I would have answers that they were not able to access. I realized that they didn't care what I believed in if I had answers that solved their problems.

I started to see that the Father loved people so much that He was willing to answer their questions even if they were not ready to receive Him—this challenged all my theology about Him then. What was interesting was that many of these people had their own encounter with the Father and I could see it. Similarly to when Peter went to the house of Cornelius because he had a vision, and the Holy Spirit fell on the Gentiles just like He had them, I'm sure it challenged what he believed. I went with Him on this journey and began to realize this was His modus operandi. I then started to look for what and with whom He was engaging through His answers. It takes time to develop yourself so that you will cooperate with the Father. This process is about you growing up in Him, discovering who He is and who you are in Him, and finding the beauty He put in you that will enable people to find Him.

Developing yourself and learning how to allow His answers to flow through you will enable you to have influence with people. His answers and influence are given as you grow up. Like Jesus, you must be tested before the ring and robe of the Father is given to you. Then the beauty He placed in you will flow as He intended. I believe that in order to walk out who you are, you must mature and grow in the Kingdom of God. As long as we stay immature or unaware of what He wants to do through us, it won't happen. Galatians 4:1 says, "Now I say that the heir, as long as he is a child, does not differ at all from a slave though he is master of all." We can see that our growth and becoming has a lot to do with whether we walk in our full inheritance that He provided.

The tension for us is really how powerful He has made us. Because of fear or deception, the church has backed away from embracing our true identity with the Father—the work of identification that was done through Jesus. He became everything we were so that we could become everything He is (see 1 John 4:17). This places us in a state of being joint heirs with him, meaning 'same.' The tension comes as our identity grows and we become powerful and gain influence through the beauty and answers that flows through us. You will gain not only power and influence, but also wealth through this process. The question then becomes: will we now believe it is our power and hands that created it? Or will we know that it's His? Will we corrupt the wisdom or abuse the beauty, such as Lucifer did? Or rise higher because we realize it's from the Father? Sonship is walked-out and matured-in as we grow up in Him. Also 1 John 2:11-14 gives us a picture of how our maturity as sons is developed. He mentions children, young men, and fathers in this passage. This is the process we go through. Sometimes it takes 25 years to be an overnight success.

But he that hateth his brother is in darkness, and walketh in darkness, and knoweth not whither he goeth, because that darkness hath blinded his eyes. I write unto you, little children, because your sins are forgiven you for his name's sake. I write unto you, fathers, because ye have known him that is from the beginning. I write unto you, young men, because ye have overcome the wicked one. I write unto you, little children, because ye have known the Father. I have written unto you, fathers, because

ye have known him that is from the beginning.
I have written unto you, young men, because ye
are strong, and the word of God abideth in you,
and ye have overcome the wicked one.
— 1 John 2:11-14

The question is: can you manage yourself when He starts to pour out His blessings upon you? Will you still realize that His image and beauty is what you carry? Will you remain a son or not? Maybe you will explore the path of an orphan, like Lucifer, and start to think it's *your* glory and power that has produced the wealth in your life?

We must get our identity back without forgetting where it came from and who we are in Him. Some of what you've read in this book has probably caused you to question my theology, and ask if what's here is from God. As I bring the book to a close, I will say that I'm a son—meaning one with the Father and Jesus, but I am not the Father. If we keep this separation, we won't make the same horrific error that Lucifer made.

The robe and the ring given to us is to bring His Kingdom to earth and disciple the nations with His values. He has given through inheritance what we couldn't earn or accomplish through our strength, because we are His sons and daughters called to rescue and restore the world. He wants you to begin to mature so we will serve and govern with the Father's intention, which is to save the systems and people He loves. We must regain our identity in who He made us so that we can start to rise in this time. Creation is watching and waiting for the sons of God to fix what is broken, restore and rescue that, which is living below His standard.

Will we allow our beauty to once again rise so that the world will have something to look at that represents His Beauty? He is the Desire of nations, Lily of the valley, Fairest among ten thousand, Lion of the tribe of Judah, and the Hope of the world! We must allow His Beauty to flow over ours so that all creation can see Him. With our heart toward Him and our life in His hands, let us at once rise up and step into the place that He gave us through inheritance. Let us begin to restore and rescue what we see is broken, because we have stayed on the sideline far too long! As David said, "Is there not a cause?" How long will we see the world Jesus gave everything for be destroyed by darkness? Let us as sons and daughters begin the process of setting things right, that Jesus will get His full reward. Amen!

ABOUT DON W. LONG

Don W. Long's greatest passion is leading others to step into their authentic identity, unleash the power within, and live their boldest life. He believes everyone was born with a unique DNA, destiny, and purpose given by the Father, and it is living inside everyone now and it just needs to be uncov-

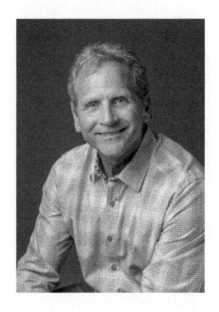

ered. Through his transformational teaching and insights, he helps people to identify and uncover who they were meant to be before they were born and helps connect them with their desires, dreams, and ultimately their destiny to live fully alive and free. He has held various leadership roles in two non-profit organizations.

Don has built two multimillion-dollar businesses, and sold one of them in the early 2000's. He then focused his energy on his primary business, and by 2017 it had risen to the top 1% of companies in the United States in that specific industry. He sold that business in 2019 for 7 figures.

Don has written an international bestselling book about sales, *Sell or Don't Eat: How Selling from the Soul Will Keep Food on Your Table,* and offers a course on sales called *Selling from the Soul.* He has been married to the love of his life, Cindy, for 37 years and has two beautiful daughters Ashton and Jordan. He currently resides in Apex, North Carolina

OTHER RESOURCES BY DON W. LONG

Don's book on Sales:

Sell or Don't Eat - sellordonteat.com

Don's signature course on Sales:

Selling from the Soul - thesellingblueprint.com

Don's audio series on building a scaling business:

Worldclass Business Systems -

worldclassbusinesssystem.com

Free audio series on applying The Blueprint of God:

The Keys for Life - lifeinstate.com

30 days of 5-minute audio lessons on business and personal growth:

Life Bites for Life - lifebitesforlife.com

Don's website

donwlong.com